LA TRAVIATA

Giuseppe Verdi

1813 - 1901

Violetta Valéry	Beverly Sills
Alfredo Germont	Nicolai Gedda
Giorgio Germont	Rolando Panerai
Flora Bervoix	Delia Wallis
Annina	Mirella Fiorentini
Gastone	Keith Erwen
Barone Douphol	Terence Sharpe
Marchese d'Obigny	Richard Van Allan
Dottore Grenvil	Robert Lloyd
Giuseppe/Servant	Mario Carlin
Commissionario	William Elvin

Conducted by Aldo Ceccato
Royal Philharmonic Orchestra
The John Alldis Choir
Chorus Master: John Alldis

La Traviata

LA TRAVIATA

Giuseppi Verdi

TEXT BY DANIEL S. BRINK

Additional commentary by William Berger

BLACK DOG
& LEVENTHAL
PUBLISHERS
NEW YORK

Published by
Black Dog & Leventhal Publishers, Inc.
151 West 19th Street
New York, NY 10011

Distributed by
Workman Publishing Company
708 Broadway
New York, NY 10003

Manufactured in China

Cover and interior design by Liz Driesbach.

Cover image © The Art Archive / Museo Teatrale alla Scala Milan / Dagli Orti

ISBN: 1-57912-507-7

h g f e d c b a

Library of Congress Cataloging-in-Publication Data available on file.

La Traviata—one of the greatest works from the most celebrated opera composers in history—is one of the mainstays of the operatic stage. Verdi achieved a magical and delicate balance between a tragic love story, a socially and politically courageous plot and some of the most powerful and heartbreaking music ever written.

You will hear the entire opera on the two compact discs included on the inside front and back covers of this book. As you explore the book, you will discover the story behind the opera and its creation, the life of the composer, biographies of the principal singers and conductor, and the opera's text, or libretto, both in Italian and English. Expert commentary has been added to the libretto to aid in your appreciation and to highlight key moments in the score.

Enjoy this book and enjoy the music.

ABOUT THE AUTHOR

*D*aniel S. Brink is the Artistic Advisor and Principal Coach/Accompanist for the Colorado Opera Festival, Artistic Director for the Company Singers, a development program for young operatic hopefuls and Artistic Director/Conductor of the Colorado Springs Choral Society small ensemble, MOSI-AC. Mr. Brink is a lecturer in Music and principal accompanist at The Colorado College, and has performed extensively in the United States and Europe. He is a highly regarded director, recitalist, teacher, adjudicator and writer.

ACKNOWLEDGEMENTS

I would like to thank Annette Megneys of the Colorado College Music Library and Jan Boothroyd, Executive Director of the Colorado Opera Festival for their invaluable assistance in researching this project. I would also like to thank my editor, Jessica MacMurray, whose influence afforded me the opportunity to write about these beloved works.

LA TRAVIATA

*G*iuseppe Verdi—the name has been synonymous with opera for a century and a half. He was born into an Italy divided under French and Austrian rule, and his work would eventually play a part in Italy's unification. His voice gave Italy a musical identity when the whole artistic world was proclaiming Richard Wagner the wave of the future. Over a sixty-year career, he gave the world 32 operas, including rewrites, which were extensive. He wrote countless other works, the most famous of which is his *Requiem*, written on the death of Alesandro Manzoni, an Italian author whose work had inspired Verdi in his youth.

He was born on October 10, 1813, in the small village of Le Roncole in northern Italy. His father, Carlo Verdi, a poor

Giuseppe Verdi (1813–1901)

Adelina Patti as Violetta, circa 1890

peasant, ran the local combination shop (an inn and tavern) and farmed a small plot of land. Verdi had only one sibling, a younger sister who was retarded and who died in her teenage years. As a child, he showed an early interest in music. It is said that he used to follow an itinerant fiddle player all around the village, and that he would be transfixed by the organ music at church on Sundays, sometimes forgetting his duties as acolyte. And sometime before his eighth birthday, Verdi's father gave him an old spinet—a small harpsichord—whose popularity had already long since been supplanted by the piano.

Carlo Verdi had dealings with Antonio Barezzi, a leading businessman in the larger town of Busseto three miles away. Barezzi owned the city's department store and was the president of the local Philharmonic Society, an amateur group which performed at local events and played concerts throughout the region. When Giuseppe was ten years old, his father and Barezzi arranged for him to go and board with a cobbler in Busseto, so that his general education could be taken over by Don Pietro Seletti, a priest at the local cathedral, and his musical education could be formalized under Ferdinando Provesi, music director at the cathedral.

The young Verdi proved himself a diligent worker, though he was more successful in his musical studies than in his other subjects. And every Sunday he walked the three miles to Le Roncole to play the organ at the village church. As Verdi's skills advanced, he composed marches and overtures for the Philharmonic Society and occasionally served as its conductor. At age 16, he moved into Barezzi's home and helped him both conduct his business affairs and coordinate his musical leadership in the city.

In 1832, it was decided that Giuseppe's talent warranted sending him to the Milan Conservatory. Milan was the musical capital of Italy and the home of La Scala, Italy's leading

Act II, Her Majesty's Theatre, London, 1856

opera house. At age 19, with the financial backing of Barezzi and a local charitable foundation, Verdi moved to Milan. However, he was not accepted at the Conservatory, and the reasons why were never given. He was sent instead to study privately with Vincenzo Lavigna, a respected conductor at La Scala, under whose tutelage Verdi thrived. Years later, when a desire was expressed to change the name of the Milan conservatory to the Verdi Conservatory, Verdi refused to grant permission, saying, "They didn't want me when I was young, they can't have me now that I'm old."

In the summer of 1833, Verdi's former mentor, Provesi, died, leaving the music director's post in Busseto open. Barezzi and the Philharmonic Society wanted Verdi for the job, while the leadership at the cathedral backed another candidate. This conflict divided the town into two camps and eventually required government intervention. In the end, Verdi won the position. The dispute had lasted three years, by which time Verdi's studies with Lavigna were completed. And his time in Milan had exposed him to the triumphs of the leading opera composers of the era—the sparkling comedies of Rossini, the masterful melodic gift of Bellini, and the seductive charm of Donizetti. He had also been presented with a libretto, *Oberto, Conte di San Bonifacio*, and had already begun work on it before he returned to Busseto to begin his new job.

With his education complete and a paying position in Busseto, he married Barezzi's eldest daughter, Margherita, with

Joan Cross as Violetta; Sadlers Wells Opera, 1941

whom he had fallen in love over the years of his close association with her father. He settled into his new job and family life, but continued to work on his opera and court the appropriate connections in Milan to see it produced. Verdi was introduced to Bartolomeo Merelli, the new impresario at La Scala, and after a long period of alternating promise and disappointment, he was granted a production of *Oberto* in the fall of 1839. The opera was a huge success and prompted Merelli to commission three more operas from Verdi. His new professional course appeared to be set, so Verdi resigned his position in Busseto and moved to Milan.

While success was the order of the day in his work, Verdi's personal life was unraveling tragically. Since their marriage, Margherita had borne Verdi two children, a daughter, Virginia, born in March of 1837, and a son, Icilio, born in July of 1838. One month and a day after Icilio's birth, Virginia suddenly died of an unidentified illness. Fourteen months later, in October of 1839, Icilio died.

Again, the cause was unknown. The young parents were horrified. Then, on June 18, 1840, Margherita died of encephalitis. Alone and devastated, Verdi pressed on through the premiere of his second opera, *Un Giorno di Regno*, the only comedy he would attempt until his final opera, *Falstaff*, debuted in 1893. *Un Giorno* was a dismal failure.

Professionally and personally defeated, Verdi wanted to stop composing and canceled his contract with Merelli, becoming a near recluse. Several months later, Verdi ran into Merelli on the street, and the impresario encouraged him to resume

Giuseppe Verdi

his work. Gradually, Verdi responded, and his next effort, *Nabucco*, a biblical epic on the Babylonian captivity of the Jews, was the overwhelmingly successful result. A particular chorus from the opera, *Va, pensiero, sull'ali dorate* (Fly, thought, on golden wings), is sung by the captive Hebrews as they recall the beauty of their homeland and long for freedom. The Milanese public, under oppressive Austrian rule, identified with the chorus's sentiment, and from the first performance it became the anthem for an Italian nation longing for independence. Many years later, at Verdi's funeral, the thousands who lined the streets began singing this chorus spontaneously as his body was carried by.

With the success of *Nabucco*, Verdi's financial worries were over. Between 1843 and 1850, he produced 13 new operas, most of which were warmly accepted by the public and critics alike. While not all of these remain in the popular repertoire today, they represent a steady growth in Verdi's musical style

and dramatic ideals. The construction of these operas owes
much to Verdi's predecessors. They are made up of a series
of "set numbers"—arias which reveal the inner thoughts of
the characters and recitatives and ensembles that advance the
dramatic action. Like Rossini, Bellini and Donizetti, the kings

Metropolitan Opera production of *La Traviata*, 1989

of the bel canto era, Verdi's primary musical tool was a gift for melody, where the orchestra plays a secondary role to the voice. (In contrast, in Wagner's music dramas, the orchestra almost becomes another character, and its contribution is essential to the dramatic flow.)

Of these early Verdi works, *Ernani, Macbeth* and perhaps *Luisa Miller* are the most frequently performed today, although all of them have received periodic revivals and even complete recordings in the past few decades. These three, however, best represent Verdi's capacity for emotional intensity and the vital, earthy quality that distinguishes his best work. Most of the operas of this period take place against the backdrop of political intrigue, and during these years Verdi had many run-ins with the Austrian censors. In the minds of the Italian people, Verdi was increasingly becoming a political figure, and lines from his operas became bywords for the resistance to Austrian occupation. In his opera, *Attila,* for example, we hear the line "*Avrai tu L'universo, resti l'Italia a me*" (You may have the rest of the world, leave Italy to me). This became the motto of the *Risorgamento,* the movement to unite Italy under one native ruler. In his *La Battaglia di Legnano,* there is a scene in which an imprisoned officer of the resistance throws himself into the river below, distraught at his inability to join his fellows in the march on the oppressor. At a performance of this opera in 1849, a soldier in the audience was so caught up in the passion of the moment that he threw himself out of the gallery and into the orchestra pit. Miraculously, no one was hurt.

Also during this period, to the annoyance of the Austrian police, the walls of most major cities in Italy were covered with graffiti saying "*Viva Verdi.*" This cry of the underground had a double meaning: First, it was for many an acknowledgment of Giuseppe Verdi as a voice for the unification movement; it was also an acrostic for "*Viva Vittorio Emmanuele, Re D'Italia*"

(Long live Victor Emmanuel, King of Italy). Vittorio Emmanuele was then king of Piedmont, the northwestern region of the peninsula, and he was thought to be a sympathetic ruler. He would eventually become king of a mostly united Italy, and reign from 1861 to 1878. For himself, Verdi remained an unwilling political hero, saying throughout his life that he knew nothing of politics. He was even pressed into service for a time as a representative from Busseto and its district to the first Italian Parliament, but thought of himself as an ill-informed and ineffectual legislator.

The intervening years also saw important developments in Verdi's personal life. Giuseppina Strepponi was a leading soprano of the time, and she had known and worked with Verdi since the beginnings of his career. Her influence was instrumental in ensuring that his first opera, *Oberto*, was staged, and she had created the leading role of Abigaille in his triumphant *Nabucco*. They had remained good friends, but sometime during the middle of the 1840s, friendship blossomed into

Alexander Dumas (1824–1895)

Act III, Metropolitan Opera, 1981

love. She had retired from the stage and was teaching in Paris, where their affair probably began. By the end of the decade, she was living with Verdi in Busseto, much to the consternation of his father-in-law and mentor, Antonio Barrezzi, his parents, and the rest of the populace of his hometown, who shunned them both. Their relationship was idyllic, however, and after an inexplicable wait of over ten years, they were married in 1859. She remained his indispensable lover, helpmate and confidante for the rest of their lives. She died in 1897, a year and a half before Verdi's death.

In 1848, Verdi purchased his sprawling estate at Sant'Agata. This was to be his home and haven for the rest of his life.

Over the years, he had become a shrewd businessman, carefully overseeing the contracts for performances of all his works. Now he applied those same skills to the occupation of his ancestors, running a large and very successful farm in what was, at first glance, a flat and forbidding landscape. He studied modern farming techniques to improve the yield of the soil, and he contributed much to the area's depressed economy by employing many of the local peasants with whom he dealt generously. Through the years, farming proved to be an even greater passion for Verdi than music, and it contributed greatly to his wealth. He always thought of himself as a simple man from the country, and it was in this environment that his creative energies were most acute.

The years from 1850 to 1853 saw the creation of three of Verdi's most enduring works, *Rigoletto, Il Trovatore* and *La Traviata.* Until these operas, the characters to whom Verdi was attracted were mainly historical and monochromatic. A character was either all good or all bad, and Verdi's capacity to represent that in musical terms had developed well. Now, however, he actively sought enigmatic characters, ones who were both hostile and loving, hero and outcast. As a result, the way in which Verdi structured his operas underwent a change. Where his basic unit of construction had always been the aria, now it became the scene, and the result was heightened dramatic effect.

Rigoletto was based on Victor Hugo's *Le Roi S'Amuse (The King Amuses Himself).* During its preparation, Verdi had no end of troubles with the censors, who initially banned the

Maria Callas as Violetta, 1958

libretto altogether. They no doubt thought the corrupt king in the story could all too easily be equated in the public mind with any number of the current Italian leaders placed in power by Austria. Through lengthy negotiation, Verdi was able to gain approval for the libretto, after changing the characters's names and the time and locale of the action, But he then had only 40 days to complete the score prior to its scheduled premiere.

Rigoletto is the story of a deformed jester whose beloved daughter is seduced by the libertine duke in whose court the jester entertains. Seeking revenge, he hires an assassin to kill the duke. Instead, the jester's daughter is accidentally killed as she attempts to save the duke who has loved her and left her. This work was an exceptionally lurid tale for the Italian stage at that time. Rigoletto, the hunchback jester, is both a loving father and an attempted murderer. Gilda, his daughter (who was raped), sacrifices her life for her rapist, and the decadent duke gets off scot-free. There are no unqualified heroes or completely innocent victims here, and it was a challenge to the moral sensibilities of the day. Still, the public was enthralled, though the critics dutifully objected to the subject matter.

Verdi's next endeavor was to set *El Trovador*, a Spanish drama by Gutierrez. It is a dark and complex story centered on the gypsy, Azucena. She is driven both by her vendetta against the Count di Luna and by her all-consuming love for her son, Manrico. This dual nature and moral ambiguity, as in the character of Rigoletto, was attractive to Verdi. He was very keen on maintaining the intensity of the Spanish version and rejected the work of his librettists several times during the creative

process. What resulted was a taut little drama with a wealth of deeply passionate music, though much of the real action of the story takes place offstage. The opera, *Il Trovatore*, opened in Rome on January 19, 1853, and was an unqualified success. It immediately began to be produced all over the operatic world.

Nicolai Gedda as Alfredo

In the winter of 1851–52, while he was working on *Il Trova-tore* for its Roman debut, Verdi and Strepponi went to Paris. There, he saw "La Dame aux Camélias," a new play by Alexandre Dumas fils, based on the author's 1848 novel, *Camille.* Verdi may have been familiar with the widely read novel, as well as with the play, which was the rage in Paris. It was the character of Camille—called Violetta in the opera—that piqued Verdi's interest. Like the hunchback, Rigoletto, and the Gypsy, Azucena, the courtesan Violetta was a figure that would be shunned by polite society. Yet she is ennobled by her capacity for loving self-sacrifice. Verdi immediately commissioned a libretto from Francesco Maria Piave, who had contributed the verses for six of his previous operas including the highly esteemed *Macbeth* and *Rigoletto.* The opera, *La Traviata,* would be produced on March 6, 1853, at the Teatro La Fenice in Venice, only seven weeks after the world was first introduced to *Il Trovatore* in Rome.

Verdi spent the bulk of 1852 working on *Il Trovatore* and *La Traviata* concurrently. After his stay in Rome for the preparation and premiere of *Il Trovatore,* he returned to Busseto. There he received disturbing news from a friend in Venice. Fanny Salvini-Donatelli, the soprano who he had hired to create the role of Violetta, had been giving some substandard performances, and Verdi was warned that her work might mar the premiere of *La Traviata.* Writing quickly to Venice,

Act II, Scene II, guests masquerading at Flora's party.
Glyndebourne Festival Opera

Verdi requested the role be recast, but the soprano he preferred was unavailable, and it was contractually too late to search for another.

Verdi arrived in Venice only 13 days prior to the premiere. It had been his custom to arrive several weeks before an opening and meticulously oversee every facet of rehearsal and production. He also usually spent these final weeks orchestrating the new work, never promising the orchestral parts in the contract until the day before the final rehearsal. It is possible, in this case, that these last 13 days were actually spent feverishly orchestrating the score, and Verdi had no time to attend rehearsals. There is no correspondence from the time that recorded how he spent his time or what his reactions were to the preparation of his new work.

The premiere was a complete fiasco. The audience, polite at first, was increasingly cool as the opera progressed, and during the final act, in which Violetta is dying of consumption, there was continuous laughter. It seems that Salvini-Donatelli was not only the picture of health but rather plump, and her persistent cough became a source of comic relief rather than pathos. The critics acknowledged that the singers were most of the problem. The tenor singing the role of Violetta's lover, Alfredo, was losing his voice, and the baritone, in the role of Alfredo's father, Germont, put nothing into his performance. He had been the creator of the plum role of *Rigoletto* and was a well-known interpreter of the title role in Verdi's *Macbeth*, so the smaller, less pivotal role of Germont seem to him too inconsequential to warrant his careful attention.

Verdi, never one to be swayed by public opinion, was unusually cavalier about the opera's failure. The day after the opening, he dashed off a series of short notes to friends and associates. His note to a former student, Emanuele Muzio, typifies his demeanor; "Dear Emanuele: "*Traviata* last night—a fiasco. Was it my fault or the singers's? . . . Time will tell."

There is an atypical lack of correspondence from Verdi about the whole matter. The opera, originally written as a contemporary drama, was set in early 1700s for the Venice production—an alteration that Verdi would usually not have tolerated. Also, he had never been complacent about casting problems before, vehemently fighting for his rights to cast the first performances of works and even cancelling them if his wishes were not followed.

Whatever the reasons for his casual approach, *La Traviata* was simply shelved for a year, until Verdi was approached by a Signor Gallo, a violinist from Venice whose family owned a respected theatre there, the Teatro San Benedetto. He had enjoyed the opera and wanted to stage a revival at the smaller theater. On May 6, 1854, 14 months after its disastrous premiere, *La Traviata* took stage again to tremendous acclaim. Verdi mused that it was the same opera heard by the same public, and there was no accounting for the radical shift in their response. Like so many of its predecessors, it overcame a nightmarish premiere, was soon heard in all the world's major opera houses, and has remained an indispensable part of the standard repertoire to this day.

Perhaps both the opera's initial failure and ultimate success are due in part to the scandalous subject matter. Violetta, a beautiful young courtesan, abandons her lavish Parisian lifestyle for the true love of Alfredo, a penniless young man from Provence. They are blissfully happy until his father intervenes, demanding that Violetta break off the relationship, because the fiancé of the young man's sister will not marry

Dress Rehearsal, Glyndebourne Festival Opera

her while her brother's illicit union continues. Violetta agrees
and sacrifices the idyllic relationship, telling Alfredo she no
longer loves him. She returns to her empty life in Paris. In
the end, alone and dying of tuberculosis, Violetta awaits Alfredo's return. His father tells him about her noble gesture, and

Alfredo comes to be reunited with her. His appearance gives her the hope of recovery, but it is too late, and she dies in his arms.

The Italian operatic audience was accustomed to seeing human tribulation padded by the trappings of historical distance. The immediacy of presenting a modern French courtesan as a sympathetic character, whose nobility of spirit made her sacrifice her only chance at real happiness for the sake of her lover's family, was seen as an affront to the social mores of the time. Yet this same scenario was seen as vindication by those ostracized because of their lifestyles, and they rallied around the work. Verdi, who at this time was still "living in sin" with Strepponi, was one of them.

The great Giuseppe Verdi, who had for many years subtly reflected the political injustices of his homeland in his operas, now appeared to be taking on the whole social order of his time.

THE STORY OF THE OPERA

Christine Nilsson as Violetta

Act 1

Violetta Valéry, a young and beautiful courtesan, is receiving guests at a lavish party at her beautiful Paris home. She warmly greets her dearest friend, Flora and her escort, the Marquis, who express concern about her capacity to host such a party, as she has recently been quite ill. Violetta responds with her personal philosophy, saying that she gives her life over to pleasure, and that pleasure is the best medicine for her ills.

Another friend, Viscount Gaston de Letorieres, enters with a friend, Alfredo Germont, a young man from Provence.

Alfredo Germont (Beniamino Prior) during the infamous *Drinking Song*, San Francisco Opera, 1980

Gaston introduces Alfredo to Violetta, telling her that the young man has long been an admirer. Violetta greets him warmly. After asking a servant if dinner is prepared, she calls on all to be seated and join in a toast. Gaston tells Violetta that during her recent illness Alfredo came to her home daily to inquire about her well-being. She is incredulous, but Gaston assures her it is true. She seeks verification from Alfredo, who admits it is true. She then teases her escort, the Baron Douphal, saying that he was nowhere near as attentive. The Baron replies that he has only known her a year, and Flora chides him for his response. The Baron then confides to Flora that he is developing a dislike for Alfredo.

Gaston invites the Baron to propose a toast, but he silently refuses. Everyone then begins coaxing Alfredo to propose a toast. He shyly asks Violetta if it would please her, and she responds that it would. Alfredo then begins a lively waltz song in praise of wine and pleasure, but especially in praise of love and the irresistible beauty of Violetta. She, in turn, sings that all, including love, is folly and that life's meaning is found in seeking pleasure.

They drink, and music is heard from an adjoining room. Violetta than invites her guests to go to the ballroom and dance. As they begin to leave the room Violetta rises to join them, but suddenly feels faint. Everyone gathers around her expressing concern, but she assures them that it is nothing and sends them in to dance, saying she will join them in a moment. All leave except Alfredo. Unaware that he is there, Violetta looks in a mirror and remarks at how pale she is. Alfredo chides her for her frivolous lifestyle, telling her she must take care of herself and that if she were his, he would take care of her. She responds that there is no one to care for her. Alfredo declares his love, but she dismisses it with a laugh. He is hurt by her response, and gradually she begins to understand that he is serious. They join in a duet in which Alfredo recounts the day he first saw her and how he has been in love with her ever since. She gently responds that she cannot love him or accept his love, that she can only offer him friendship and that he must find another love. She asks him to speak no more of love, and he replies that he will obey. She tenderly gives him a flower from her bosom, asking him to return it when it has

Chorus members of the San Francisco Opera celebrate a festive evening, Act I.

withered. "Tomorrow?" he asks. "Yes," she replies. They gently say good-bye, and Alfredo kisses her hand and leaves.

The guests reenter, noting that dawn is breaking and they must go. They all thank Violetta for her hospitality and gradually leave the house.

Alone, Violetta reflects on the profound affect Alfredo's declaration of love has had on her. Could this be what she has always longed for? Could she really escape her lonely and meaningless existence? But her pensive and hopeful mood changes abruptly. She declares that a meaningful love for her is folly, and she must continue to follow her frantic pursuit of pleasure until she dies. She stops short as she hears

Alfredo's voice from under her balcony, repeating his ardent love for her. She momentarily reconsiders his sincerity, but quickly returns to her assertion that she must be always free and ends the Act in a florid affirmation of the lifestyle she has chosen.

Act 2

SCENE ONE

We are in the drawing room of the country home where Alfredo and Violetta have come to live together. Alfredo enters in hunting attire and pauses to reflect on the wonderful life he and Violetta have shared since she left the whirlwind of her social life in Paris three months before. Together, and unmindful of the world, they have created the perfect haven of love.

Their maid, Annina, enters, dressed for travel and clearly having just returned from a trip. Alfredo asks where she has been. Reluctantly, she tells him that Violetta sent her to Paris to arrange for the sale of her belongings to support their new life together. Filled with shame at his naiveté, Alfredo vows to go to Paris and secure the funds necessary to pay their mounting debts. He departs.

Violetta enters and asks Alfredo's whereabouts. Annina simply replies that he has gone to Paris and will return by evening. Another servant enters and delivers an invitation from Flora to a dance that evening. Violetta remarks that Flora will wait for her in vain.

The servant reenters to announce that a gentleman has arrived to see Violetta. She asks the servant to show the visitor in, and the servant presents Giorgio Germont, Alfredo's father. She is startled, but graciously offers him a seat. After he sits, he rudely exclaims that his son's life is being ruined because of her. She responds indignantly and asks him to leave, but he tells her that his son plans to give her all his possessions. She tells him that can't be true and shows him the contract

Alfredo (Beniamino Prior) & Violetta (Valerie Masterson)

for the sale of all her goods. His brusque
tone abates, and he asks how a woman
capable of such nobility could have
such a negative reputation. She replies
that she loves Alfredo and has found
happiness with him. She has made
peace with her past, has repented and
has been forgiven.

Verdi, 1867

The elder Germont then tells her
the reason for his visit. He tells her of
Alfredo's sister and her impending
marriage. Her fiancé, however, will
not marry her unless Alfredo abandons his illicit affair and
returns to his family. Violetta responds that to leave Alfredo
for a time will be difficult, but she will do it. A brief separation, however, is not what Germont is requesting—he must
ask her to give him up forever. Horrified, Violetta tells him
that she cannot give Alfredo up, that she has no friends or
family, and has given up everything for his love. She also confides that she has a deadly disease and hasn't long to live.
Germont suggests that young men like his son are fickle, and
he may not always love her as he does now; since the union is
not blessed by God, she may be left alone. Violetta reflects that
her past sins will forever haunt her. Resigned, she tearfully
tells Germont she will sacrifice the one precious thing in her
life for his family's happiness. Germont comforts her, acknowl-
edging her noble gesture and the quality of love she holds for
Alfredo. He asks her if there is anything he can do for her,

Alfredo & Giorgio Germont
at Flora's party, Act II

and she in turn asks that after her death Alfredo may know of the sacrifice she made for love of him. They bid each other farewell, and Germont retires to the garden outside.

Violetta sits down, writes a farewell letter to her lover and seals it. Alfredo enters and startles her, asking to whom she is writing. She admits it was to him, but says he must read it later. He asks her if his father has come, telling her that he received a stern letter from him, but assuring her that the elder Germont will love her at first sight. She lies, telling Alfredo that his father has not come and that she should not be there when he does. Alfredo should calm him first. Weeping, Violetta declares her love for Alfredo and begs him to express his love in return. Bidding him farewell, she leaves through the garden.

Confused by her demeanor, Alfredo absentmindedly reads a few lines from a book and then notices a man in the garden. A servant enters, telling him that Violetta has left with Annina. Shortly after, a messenger enters to deliver Violetta's farewell letter. Alfredo begins to read it and with a cry of despair, he turns to find his father at the door and throws himself into his arms. Germont tries to comfort him with a tender aria recalling the beauty of Provence, where the young man was raised. Germont implores Alfredo to return to his home and be a source of pride to his family again. Alfredo, who has been sitting with his face buried in his hands, suddenly looks up in a rage. He concludes it was Baron Douphol who stole Violetta from him and promises revenge. His father begs him to abandon this madness and return home. Alfredo sees the invitation from Flora on the table and is sure he will find Violetta there. In spite of his father's efforts to stop him, he storms from the room, determined to go to Paris and retrieve Violetta.

Act 2

In the lavish salon of Flora's Paris home, she is entertaining guests. She tells the Marquis that Alfredo and Violetta are coming, but he informs her they are separated and that Violetta will be coming with Baron Douphol. Dr. Grenvil expresses his surprise, as he had seen them only yesterday and they appeared happy. A brilliant entertainment ensues in which masked guests perform as gypsies and matadors. Flora and the Marquis tease one another about imagined infidelities, and all join in the good-natured banter.

Alfredo arrives, and the guests inquire as to Violetta's whereabouts. He non-chalantly responds that he doesn't know where she is. They then invite him to play cards, and he goes to the gaming table with Gaston and other guests to play.

Violetta enters on Baron Douphol's arm. He sees Alfredo, and taking Violetta aside, demands that she not say a single word to him. Disturbed by the tense scene, Violetta is taken aside by Flora and the Doctor who quietly ask what has happened.

Meanwhile, Alfredo is winning at cards. He loudly boasts that one unlucky in love is lucky at cards, and that his winnings

Alfredo (Beniamino Prior) sings of his broken heart

will allow him to return to the country with the one who left him. The Baron challenges him to a game. Alfredo wins the first hand. Angrily, the Baron doubles the stakes. Alfredo wins again. The tension is broken by a servant announcing that dinner is served. Alfredo offers to continue the play, but the Baron answers that they will continue later. They all exit to the dining room.

Violetta quickly returns. She has asked Alfredo to come back to the salon so she can warn him against angering the Baron further. Alfredo enters the salon and disdainfully asks what Violetta wants. She tells him that she fears a duel, and if Alfredo should be killed, she would die. He arrogantly says he would cut the Baron down, and he asks her why she should care what happens to him. She begs him to leave. He responds that he will go only if she will follow. She confesses she has taken an oath not to stay with him. Alfredo demands to know who would make her take such an oath. Was it Douphol? Lying, Violetta answers, "Yes." Alfredo asks if she loves Douphol. Again, she lies, "Yes."

Infuriated, Alfredo runs to the door, calling all the guests back into the salon. They rush into the room, and Alfredo imperiously asks if they know this woman, who was once willing to sell all she had for love of him. He then declares that he will clear himself of the stain of this dishonor and repay what he owes her in full. He hurls his winnings at her feet. Humiliated, Violetta faints in Flora's arms.

The guests, horrified at Alfredo's actions, deride his insensitivity and demand that he leave at once. His father has arrived to witness the scene and expresses his contempt for his son's actions. Suddenly aware of what he has done, Alfredo comes to his senses and timidly expresses his remorse, arguing that he was driven to madness by the loss of his love. In a moving ensemble, all present express their various feelings: the Baron reviling Alfredo for his actions; the guests sympathizing with Violetta; and Germont, in an aside, reflecting on Violetta's virtue and faithfulness, about which only he truly knows. Violetta's voice soars above the ensemble as she expresses the hope that some day Alfredo will know the depth and breadth of her love for him. The Baron challenges Alfredo to a duel, and the remorseful young man is led away by his father.

Act 3

Violetta lies dying in her semi-darkened bedroom. Annina sits sleeping in a chair near her mistress's bed. Violetta awakens and requests some water, which Annina brings her. She then asks Annina to open the shutters. As she does, she sees Dr. Grenvil arriving in the street below. Violetta comments on what a faithful friend he has been and asks Annina's help in getting up to receive him. With difficulty, Annina helps Violetta to a nearby sofa, and upon entering, the doctor helps to make her comfortable.

He asks how she is feeling, and she responds that though she is suffering, she is at peace. The priest has been there to visit her, and he was most comforting. The doctor assures her that she will be feeling better soon. As he leaves, Annina asks about Violetta's condition, and the doctor tells her that she has only hours to live.

Annina returns to Violetta, offering encouragement. Violetta inquires if it is a holiday, and Annina tells her it is Carnival, and all of Paris is going mad. She then asks the maid how much money is left, and Annina replies they have 20 louis.

Violetta (Marie McLaughlin) in her final moments

Violetta instructs her to give ten to the poor, and when Annina suggests that won't leave them with much, Violetta assures her that it will be enough. She asks for her letters, then sends Annina away to make the donation.

Violetta opens a letter from Alfredo's father which she reads aloud. He tells her that the Baron was wounded in the duel, but is recovering. He also relates that Alfredo is abroad, but that he has been told of her sacrifice and is coming with his father to beg her forgiveness. The letter closes with his wishes for her happy future. It is, however, too late.

Violetta waits for Alfredo and his father, but they don't come. She looks in a mirror and sees how her disease has ravaged her. She mourns the loss of her happy love and says that her grave will be unmarked and unadorned by flowers or tears. She prays for God's forgiveness and desperately asks that she may come to Him.

As her soliloquy ends, Violetta hears the sound of revelers in the street. Annina enters and tries to keep her calm as she tells her that Alfredo is coming. He enters and they embrace ecstatically. He reaffirms his love and begs her forgiveness. She responds that there is nothing to forgive. Now they are together and nothing will separate them again. Alfredo paints an ideal picture of their future together. They will leave Paris for the country, they will make up for all their heartaches, her health will return and they will live together always in perfect bliss. In a euphoric trance, Violetta repeats his vision.

Strengthened by her joy, Violetta rises to her feet, saying they must go to church and give thanks for their reunion, but she

Violetta & Alfredo,
reunited

falters and collapses into a chair. Alarmed, Alfredo supports her, but she attempts to rally again, asking Annina to bring her dress. Unable even to dress herself, Violetta falls back in defeat, cursing her weakness. In a panic, Alfredo sends Annina for the doctor and Violetta repeats the command, telling Annina to inform the doctor that her love has returned, and she must live again.

The maid leaves, and Violetta tells Alfredo that if his return cannot make her live, nothing can. As Alfredo attempts to calm her, she bewails the loss of her young life and all her hopes for happiness. Then Alfredo's father enters, and Violetta greets him warmly. He tells her he has come to welcome her as his daughter. But with a gentle embrace, she tells him it is too late. The doctor enters, and Violetta tells him she is dying in the presence of those she loves. Realizing that her death is imminent, Germont is stricken with remorse for having caused the separation of the two lovers.

Violetta then takes a small medallion from a drawer. It is a portrait of herself which she gives to Alfredo so that he may remember her. She tells him that he will love again, and when he does, he should give the medallion to his love and tell her that it is a portrait of one who is in heaven, praying for their happiness. As Violetta repeats these sentiments, all present pour out their grief over her impending death. Suddenly, there is a change in her demeanor. She rises and says the pain is gone, that she is reviving. She is overcome with joy. Then just as suddenly, she falls lifeless on the sofa. Dr. Grenvil rushes to check her condition and confirms that she is gone while Alfredo, Germont and Annina cry out in despair.

LA TRAVIATA

Giuseppe Verdi
1813 - 1901

Violetta Valéry	Beverly Sills
Alfredo Germont	Nicolai Gedda
Giorgio Germont	Rolando Panerai
Flora Bervoix	Delia Wallis
Annina	Mirella Fiorentini
Gastone	Keith Erwen
Barone Douphol	Terence Sharpe
Marchese d'Obigny	Richard Van Allan
Dottore Grenvil	Robert Lloyd
Giuseppe/Servant	Mario Carlin
Commissionario	William Elvin

Conducted by Aldo Ceccato
Royal Philharmonic Orchestra
The John Alldis Choir
Chorus Master: John Alldis

THE PERFORMERS

BEVERLY SILLS (Violetta Valèry) is one of the most amazing personalities ever to grace the operatic stage. For 50 years her presence has been felt throughout the world of opera and beyond. Born Belle Silverman in Brooklyn, she was a child star by the age of three and a fixture on New York radio until the age of twelve, when she "retired" to focus on her studies. These included Italian, French, and piano lessons, and voice lessons with the esteemed vocal pedagogue, Estelle Liebling. At the age of sixteen, Sills toured in operetta with the Schubert Opera Company, and a year later debuted with the Philadelphia Civic Opera and the esteemed San Francisco Opera Company.

In 1955 Sills joined the New York City Opera, achieving an early triumph in the New York premiere of Douglas Moore's *The Ballad of Baby Doe*. She continued with the company in leading roles, including all three heroines in Offenbach's *The Tales of Hoffman* in 1965. In 1966 she portrayed Cleopatra in Handel's *Giulio Cesare* to such unprecedented acclaim that it launched her international career.

Beverly Sills and her daughter, who is deaf.

In short order Sills conquered the operatic capitals of Europe, singing Mozart's "Queen of the Night" in *The Magic Flute* in Vienna, Pamira in Rossini's *The Siege of Corinth* at Milan's La Scala and the title role in Donizetti's *Lucia di Lammermoor* at Covent Garden. In the early 1970s, she sang all three of Donizetti's Tudor queens—*Maria Stuarda, Anna Bolena,* and *Elisabeth I* in *Roberto Deveraux* for her home company. These established her as one of the undisputed queens of bel canto in this century, and in 1975 she debuted at the Metropolitan Opera House as Pamira in Rossini's *The Siege of Corinth.*

Sills's repertoire encompasses more than 50 roles, from the Baroque rarity of Rameau's *Hippolyte et Aricie* to the twelve-tone intricacies of Nono's *Intolleranza*—and everything in between. One of her most famous portrayals was as Massanet's *Manon*, a work somewhat outside the mainstream of her standard fare. During her singing career she also did much to advance the cause of opera in America with her appearances on popular TV talk shows and in television specials, one of the most memorable of which paired her with the musical theater artist, Julie Andrews.

After retiring from the stage, Sills became General Director of the New York City Opera which she ran with distinction from 1979–89. Today she presides over the Board of Directors of Lincoln Center in New York, the premiere performing arts center in the nation. In 1980 she received the Presidential Medal of Freedom, and in 1985, a Kennedy Center Honor.

The role of Violetta holds a special place in Beverly Sills's heart. It was her first leading role as an aspiring young artist, one she performed countless times on tour, and it was also the vehicle for her successful debuts in Naples, Berlin and Venice. Early in life, she acquired the nickname "Bubbles," a name which reflects her ingratiating personality and a vocal quality which is so evident in this portrayal. Her unparalleled coloratura is dazzling in her first-act aria, *Sempre libera*, and the warmth of her second-act self-denial is heartrending. Her incredible acting skill is apparent in the careful handling of her third-act decline, in which the aria *Addio del passato* is particularly moving. In this recording we are treated to the broad vocal and dramatic range of one of the greatest ladies of the operatic stage.

NICOLAI GEDDA (Alfredo Germont) is widely regarded as having one of the most beautiful tenor voices of the century. He is frequently pointed to as the best possible model for young singers, who learn by listening to the integrity of his pitch, the beauty of his vocal lines and the ease of his technique. Also one of the most intelligent operatic artists of the century, he speaks and sings fluently in seven languages.

Gedda was born in Stockholm, the son of a Swedish mother and a Russian father. After leaving school he began a career in banking, but with the help of a client was able to begin vocal studies with the Swedish tenor, Carl Martin Oehman. After winning the Christine Nilsson Award, Gedda studied at the Royal Conservatory of Music in Stockholm.

He made his operatic debut in 1952 in *Le Postillon de Lonjumeau* at the Royal Opera House in Stockholm. Only months later, Gedda was hired to record the role of Dmitri the Pretender in Mussorgsky's *Boris Godunov*, and his future was secured. In 1953 he debuted at La Scala as Don Ottavio in Mozart's *Don Giovanni* and was chosen by Carl Orff to create the role of the groom in his *Il Trionfo di Afrodite*. Over the next two years he debuted at the Paris Opera and Covent Garden, and in 1957 he made his Metropolitan Opera debut, creating the role of Anatol in Samuel Barber's *Vanessa* in his first year there, and singing there regularly for over twenty years.

In 1964 he created the leading tenor role in the American premiere of Menotti's *The Last Savage*, and in 1965 he was given the title Court Singer to the Royal Court of Sweden, an honor conferred on fewer than 12 artists in 200 years.

The scope of Gedda's repertoire is unsurpassed, including over 200 works in the concert and operatic repertoire. He is equally at home as Lensky in Tchaikovsky's *Eugene Onegin* or singing an English folk song. His extensive discography includes almost 40 complete opera recordings in six languages, encompassing both lyric and dramatic roles and affording him the honor of being the most recorded tenor alive. He remains active today, mainly as a recitalist and in concert, and his recording career has continued into the 1990s.

The role of Alfredo is perfectly suited to Gedda's voice, and he is at his lyric best in this recording, handling the intimacy of *De miei bollenti spiriti* and the bravado of the frequently omitted second-act cabaletta with equal aplomb.

ROLANDO PANERAI (Giorgio Germont) was born in the small town of Campi Bisenzio near Florence. He pursued his vocal studies in Florence and Milan and made his debut in 1946 in Florence as Enrico Ashton in Donizetti's *Lucia di Lammermoor*. Over the following two years he appeared regularly in Naples where he debuted as Pharoah in Rossini's *Mosé in Egitto*. In 1951 he made his La Scala debut as the high priest in Saint-Saëns's *Samson et Dalila*. He appeared there regularly for a

Swedish tenor Nicolai Gedda

number of years, singing such diverse roles as Appolo in Gluck's *Alceste* and the husband in Menotti's comedy, *Amelia al Ballo*. In 1957 he sang the title role in the Italian premiere of Hindemith's *Mathis der Maler* at La Scala, and in 1962 he created the title role in Turchi's *Il Buon Soldato Svejk* there.

Panerai's international career began in 1955 when he created the role of Ruprecht in Prokofiev's *The Fiery Angel* in Aix-en-Provence, where he also portrayed Mozart's Figaro. He debuted in Salzburg in 1957 as Ford in Verdi's *Falstaff*, and his American debut was with the San Francisco Opera in 1958, where he sang both the Rossini and Mozart Figaros and Marcello in Puccini's *La Bohème*. His career has included all the major houses in Italy, Great Britain, France, Germany and the United States, including the Metropolitan Opera in New York. He remains active today; two of his latest specialties are the title roles in Verdi's *Falstaff* and Puccini's *Gianni Schicchi*.

Panerai's extensive discography includes over twenty complete operas, ranging from Mozart to Wagner in the German repertoire and from Rossini to Puccini in the Italian repertoire. Panerai's Germont is an intimate paternal figure which he portrays with a consistent richness of sound and intelligent characterization. He is the perfect father to Gedda's delicate and vital Alfredo, and with the elegance of Sills's Violetta, he masterfully rounds out an ideal cast for Verdi's masterpiece.

ALDO CECCATO (the conductor), is a native of Milan who began his musical career as a successful young pianist, equally comfortable in the classical and jazz genres. He studied at the

Milan Conservatory and at Berlin's Hochschule fur Musik, where he conducted a student performance of Verdi's *Otello*. It was the concert in Milan where he conducted seven Vivaldi concerti that commanded the attention of the European musical establishment. He made his professional debut with *Don Giovanni* at Milan's Teatro Nuovo in 1964, and in 1966 he conducted the Italian premiere of Busoni's *Die Brautwahl* in Florence to critical acclaim. His early association with the famous Italian conductor-composer, Victor de Sabata, who admired the young conductor's interpretation of his tone poem *Juventu*, helped to establish demand for Ceccato's work.

His growing fame in Italy soon led to engagements in Germany, France, Britain and South America, and in 1969 Ceccato made his American debut at the Chicago Lyric Opera conducting Bellini's *I Puritani*. In 1970 he made his debut with the New York Philharmonic and went on to guest conduct all the major American orchestras. He also conquered all the major opera houses in Europe, guest conducting at Covent Garden, the Glyndebourne Festival and the Paris Opera, to name just a few. Since 1975, he has confined his activity primarily to Germany.

This *Traviata* is one of only two opera recordings under Ceccato's baton. He recorded Donizetti's *Maria Stuarda* also in 1971 and also with Beverly Sills. Known for his powerful leadership and attention to detail, Ceccato delivers an expansive reading of *La Traviata*, imbuing the genteel French setting with an unmistakably Verdian soul.

The Libretto

Act 1

PRELUDE

A drawing room in Violetta's home. In the background a door, opening to another room. There are two other lateral doors; to the left, a fireplace with a mirror over the mantel. In the centre of the room, a huge table richly laden. (Violetta is seated on a sofa, talking with Dr Grenvil and other friends. Some of her friends go to greet various guests as they arrive. Among them, the Baron and Flora, escorted by the Marquis.)

DISC NO. 1/TRACK 1

The Prelude begins with a somber theme which represents the tragedy of Violetta's illness and early death. It is a theme we will hear again at the beginning of act III. This motive gives way to the theme of Violetta's farewell to Alfredo at the end of act II, scene 1. Here it is a sad and elegant encapsulation of the heroine herself. The melody is first stated by violins and cellos (01:47), then repeated by the cellos (02:50) with a violin obbligato or countermelody above it.

DISC NO. 1/TRACK 2

The first scene opens with a lively theme that underscores the whole scene. This is real party music, reminiscent of the first scene of Verdi's previous opera, *Rigoletto*. The chorus speaks as one character throughout the opera, responding as one to the progressing action.

CORO I	**CHORUS I**
Dell'invito trascorsa è già l'ora.	You were invited for an earlier hour.
Voi tardaste.	You have come late.
CORO II	**CHORUS II**
Giocammo da Flora, e giocando quell'ore volar.	We were playing cards at Flora's, and the time passed quickly.

VIOLETTA *(va loro incontro)*
Flora, amici, la notte che resta d'altre gioie
qui fate brillar. Fra le tazze più viva è la
festa.

VIOLETTA *(going to greet them)*
Flora, my friends, the rest of the evening
will be gayer because you are here. Surely
the evening is livelier with good food and
drink?

FLORA, MARCHESE
E goder voi potrete?

FLORA, MARQUIS
And can you be lively?

VIOLETTA
Lo voglio; al piacere m'affido, ed io soglio
con tal farmaco i mali sopir.

VIOLETTA
I must be.
I give myself to pleasure, since pleasure
is the best medicine for my ills.

TUTTI
Sì, la vita s'addoppia al gioir.

ALL
Indeed, life is doubly heightened by pleasure.

(The Viscount Gastone de Letorières enters with Alfredo Germont. Servants are busily engaged at the table.)

GASTONE
In Alfredo Germont, o signora, ecco un
altro che molto v'onora; pochi amici a lui
simili sono.

GASTONE
My dear Madam, in Alfredo Germont
I present a man who greatly admires you;
few friends are so fine as he.

VIOLETTA
(Violetta dà la mano ad Alfredo, che gliela bacia.)
Mio Visconte, mercé di tal dono.

VIOLETTA
(She offers her hand to Alfredo, who kisses it.)
My dear Viscount, thank you for this gift.

MARCHESE
Caro Alfredo -

MARQUIS
My dear Alfredo -

ALFREDO
Marchese -

ALFREDO
Marquis -

(They shake hands.)

GASTONE *(ad Alfredo)*
T'ho detto:
l'amistà qui s'intreccia al diletto.

GASTONE *(to Alfredo)*
As I told you,
here friendship joins with pleasure.

(Meanwhile the servants have finished setting the table.)

VIOLETTA
Pronto è il tutto?
(Un servo fa cenno di sì.)
Miei cari, sedete:
è al convito che s'apre ogni cor.

VIOLETTA
Is everything ready?
(A servant nods in affirmation.)
Please be seated:
it is at table that the heart is gayest.

TUTTI
Ben diceste - le cure segrete fuga sempre
l'amico licor.

ALL
Well spoken - secret cares fly before that
great friend, wine.

(They take their places at the table. Violetta is seated between Alfredo and Gastone. Facing her Flora takes her place between the Marquis and the Baron. The remaining guests take their various places around the table. A moment of silence as the food is served. Violetta and Gastone are whispering to each other.)

È al convito che s'apre ogni cor.

It is at table that the heart is gayest.

GASTONE
Sempre Alfredo a voi pensa.

GASTONE
Alfredo thinks of you always.

VIOLETTA
Scherzate?

VIOLETTA
You are joking?

GASTONE
Egra foste, e ogni dì con affanno qui volò,
di voi chiese.

GASTONE
While you were ill, every day he called
to ask about you.

VIOLETTA
Cessate. Nulla son io per lui.

VIOLETTA
Don't talk like that. I am nothing to him.

GASTONE

Non v'inganno.

VIOLETTA

Vero è dunque? Onde ciò?
Nol comprendo.

ALFREDO

Sì, egli è ver.

VIOLETTA

Le mie grazie vi rendo.
Voi, barone, non faceste altrettanto.

BARONE

Vi conosco da un anno soltanto.

VIOLETTA

Ed ei solo da qualche minuto.

FLORA *(sottovoce al Barone)*

Meglio fora se aveste taciuto.

BARONE *(piano a Flora)*

M'è increscioso quel giovin.

FLORA

Perché? A me invece simpatico egli è.

GASTONE *(ad Alfredo)*

E tu dunque non apri più bocca?

MARCHESE *(a Violetta)*

È a madama che scuoterlo tocca.

GASTONE

I do not deceive you.

VIOLETTA

It is true then? But why?
I don't understand.

ALFREDO

Yes, it is true.

VIOLETTA

I thank you.
You, Baron, were less attentive.

BARON

I have only known you for a year.

VIOLETTA

And he for just a few minutes.

FLORA *(in a low voice, to the Baron)*

It would have been better to say nothing.

BARON *(softly, to Flora)*

I don't like this young man.

FLORA

Why not? I think he's very pleasant.

GASTONE *(to Alfredo)*

And you have nothing more to say?

MARQUIS *(to Violetta)*

It's up to you to make him talk.

VIOLETTA
Sarò l'Ebe che versa.

ALFREDO
E ch'io bramo immortal come quella.

TUTTI
Beviamo.

GASTONE
O barone, né un verso, né un viva troverete in quest'òra giuliva?

(The Baron shakes his head.)

Dunque a te -

(nodding to Alfredo)

TUTTI
Sì, sì, un brindisi.

ALFREDO
L'estro non m'arride.

GASTONE
E non sei tu maestro?

ALFREDO *(a Violetta)*
Vi fia grato?

VIOLETTA
Sì.

ALFREDO *(s'alza)*
Sì? L'ho già in cor.

VIOLETTA
I shall be Hebe, the cup-bearer.

ALFREDO
And, like her, immortal, I hope.

ALL
Let us drink.

GASTONE
Baron - can't you find a toast for this happy occasion?

Then it's up to you -

ALL
Yes, yes, a toast.

ALFREDO
Inspiration fails me.

GASTONE
But aren't you a master?

ALFREDO *(to Violetta)*
Would it please you?

VIOLETTA
Yes.

ALFREDO *(rising)*
Yes? I have it already in my heart.

MARCHESE	MARQUIS
Dunque attenti!	Then - attention!

TUTTI	ALL
Sì, attenti al cantor.	Yes, to the poet.

DISC NO. 1/TRACK 3

Libiamo is one of the most famous "drinking songs" in the operatic repertoire. Its lusty waltz rhythm is a favorite of opera lovers, and it is frequently extracted and performed outside the opera. Within the drama, the swirling melody perfectly describes the giddy social rounds of the Parisian party circuit.

ALFREDO	ALFREDO
Libiamo, ne' lieti calici	Drink from the joyful glass,
che la bellezza infiora,	resplendent with beauty,
e la fuggevol ora	drink to the spirit of pleasure
s'inebrii a voluttà.	which enchants the fleeting moment.
Libiam ne' dolci fremiti	Drink to the thrilling sweetness
che suscita l'amore,	brought to us by love,
poiché quell'occhio al core	for these fair eyes, irresistibly,
(indicando Violetta)	*(indicating Violetta)*
onnipotente va.	pierce us to the heart.
Libiamo amore, amor fra i calici	Drink - for wine
più caldi baci avrà.	will warm the kisses of love.

TUTTI	ALL
Ah! Libiam, amor fra i calici	Drink - for wine
più caldi baci avrà.	will warm the kisses of love.

VIOLETTA *(s'alza)*	VIOLETTA *(rising)*
Tra voi saprò dividere	I shall divide my gaiety
il tempo mio giocondo;	among you all;
tutto è follia nel mondo	Everything in life is folly,
ciò che non è piacer.	except for pleasure.
Godiam, fugace e rapido	Let us be joyful, for love

è il gaudio dell'amore,
è un fior che nasce e muore,
né più si può goder.
Godiam, c'invita un fervido
accento lusinghier.

TUTTI
Ah! godiamo, la tazza e il cantico
la notte abbella e il riso;
in questo paradiso
ne scopra il nuovo dì.

VIOLETTA (ad Alfredo)
La vita è nel tripudio.

ALFREDO (a Violetta)
Quando non s'ami ancora.

VIOLETTA
Nol dite a chi l'ignora.

ALFREDO
È il mio destin così.

TUTTI
Godiamo, la tazza e il cantico
la notte abbella e il riso;
in questo paradiso
ne scopra il nuovo dì.

is a fleeting and short-lived joy.
A flower which blossoms and fades,
whose beauty is soon lost forever.
Be joyful - a caressing voice
invites us warmly to joy.

ALL
Ah! Be carefree - for wine and song
with laughter, embellish the night.
The new day breaking will find us still
in this happy paradise.

VIOLETTA (to Alfredo)
Life is only pleasure.

ALFREDO (to Violetta)
For those who don't know love.

VIOLETTA
Speak not of love to one who knows not
what it is.

ALFREDO
Such is my destiny.

ALL
Be carefree - for wine and song
with laughter, embellish the night.
The next day breaking will find us still
in this happy paradise.

(The sound of music is heard, coming from an adjoining room.)

Reknowned soprano Mirella Freni, as Violetta

In this section, Violetta's and Alfredo's exchanges are heard in relief against the background dance music. She is keeping up a brave front at this point, both about her illness and her vulnerability to true love.

Che è ciò?	What is that?

VIOLETTA	**VIOLETTA**
Non gradireste ora le danze?	Wouldn't you like to dance now?

TUTTI	**ALL**
Oh, il gentil pensier! Tutti accettiamo.	How kind of you! We accept with pleasure.

VIOLETTA	**VIOLETTA**
Usciamo dunque.	Let us go, then.

(As they are going out through the centre door, Violetta suddenly turns pale.)

Ohimè!	Oh!

TUTTI	**ALL**
Che avete?	What is the matter?

VIOLETTA	**VIOLETTA**
Nulla, nulla.	Nothing, it is nothing.

TUTTI	**ALL**
Che mai v'arresta?	Why have you stopped here?

VIOLETTA	**VIOLETTA**
Usciamo.	Let us go out.

(She takes a few steps, but then is forced to stop again and to sit down.)

Oh Dio!	Oh God!

TUTTI	ALL
Ancora!	Again!

ALFREDO	ALFREDO
Voi soffrite?	Are you ill?

TUTTI	ALL
Oh ciel! Ch'è questo?	Heavens, what can it be?

VIOLETTA	VIOLETTA
Un tremito che provo.	It's just a chill.
Or là passate.	Go on - please - there.

(She points towards the other room.)

Fra poco anch'io sarò.	In just a few minutes I shall come -

TUTTI	ALL
Come bramate.	As you wish.

(All except Alfredo go into the other room.)

VIOLETTA *(Si alza e va a guardarsi allo specchio.)* Oh, qual pallor!	**VIOLETTA** *(looking into a mirror)* How pale I am!

(turning she sees Alfredo)

Voi qui.	You are here!

ALFREDO	ALFREDO
Cessata è l'ansia che vi turbò?	Are you feeling better now?

VIOLETTA	VIOLETTA
Sto meglio.	Yes, better, thank you.

Violetta & Alfredo (Beniamino Prior & Valerie Masterson)

ALFREDO

Ah, in cotal guisa v'ucciderete - aver v'è
d'uopo cura dell'esser vostro -

VIOLETTA

E lo potrei?

ALFREDO

Oh, se mia foste,
custode io veglierei pe' vostri soavi dì.

VIOLETTA

Che dite? Ha forse alcuno
cura di me?

ALFREDO (con passione)

Perché nessuno al mondo v'ama.

VIOLETTA

Nessun?

ALFREDO

Tranne sol io.

VIOLETTA

Gli è vero. Sì grande amore dimenticato
avea.

ALFREDO

Ridete? E in voi v'ha un core?

VIOLETTA

Un cor? Sì, forse… e a che lo richiedete?

ALFREDO

Ah, se ciò fosse. Non potreste allora celiar.

ALFREDO

Ah, this way you will kill yourself -
you must take care of yourself -

VIOLETTA

But can I?

ALFREDO

If you were mine,
I should watch over you.

VIOLETTA

What are you saying? Is there anyone
to care for me?

ALFREDO (passionately)

That's because no one in the world loves you -

VIOLETTA

No one?

ALFREDO

Except me.

VIOLETTA

It's true! I had forgotten this great love.

ALFREDO

You laugh? Have you no heart?

VIOLETTA

A heart? Yes, perhaps - but why do you ask?

ALFREDO

Ah, if that were so, then you couldn't laugh
at me.

VIOLETTA	VIOLETTA
Dite davvero?	Are you serious?

ALFREDO	ALFREDO
Io non v'inganno.	I do not deceive you.

VIOLETTA	VIOLETTA
Da molto è che mi amate?	Have you been in love with me for long?

DISC NO.1/TRACK 5

Un dì felice, eterea. **In this intimate duet, Alfredo recalls his sight of Violetta and rhapsodizes about his love for her. Soon (00:39) his halting, self-conscious phrases expand into a lush melody that comes to represent their love and which reappears throughout the opera.**

ALFREDO

Ah, sì; da un anno.
Un dì felice, eterea,
mi balenaste innante,
e da quel dì tremante
vissi d'ignoto amor,
di quell'amor ch'è palpito
dell'universo intero,
misterioso, altero,
croce e delizia al cor.

ALFREDO

Yes, for a year.
One day you passed before me,
happy and light as air,
and ever since that day,
even without knowing it, I loved you -
with that love which is the very breath
of the universe itself -
mysterious and noble,
both cross and ecstasy of the heart.

VIOLETTA

Ah, se ciò è ver, fuggitemi.
Solo amistade io v'offro:
amar non so, nè soffro
un così eroico amore.
Io sono franca, ingenua;
altra cercar dovete;
non arduo troverete
dimenticarmi allor.

VIOLETTA

Ah, if this is true, then leave me -
I offer you only friendship:
I cannot love, nor can I accept
so heroic a love from you.
I am simple and frank.
You must find another.
It won't be hard, then,
for you to forget me.

ALFREDO

Ah, amore misterioso, altero,
croce e delizia al cor.

ALFREDO

Love mysterious and noble,
both cross and ecstasy of the heart.

VIOLETTA

Non arduo troverete dimenticarmi allor.

VIOLETTA

It won't be hard, then, for you to forget me.

DISC NO. 1/TRACK 6

The party and its music literally burst in on Violetta's private moment with Alfredo, as Gastone opens the door. Violetta's dialogue with Alfredo suggests other, more personal, doors are opening as well.

GASTONE *(sulla porta di mezzo)*
Ebben? Che diavol fate?

GASTONE *(in the doorway)*
Well, now? What the devil are you doing?

VIOLETTA
Si folleggiava.

VIOLETTA
We were joking.

GASTONE
Ah, ah! Sta ben - restate.

GASTONE
Aha! Good! Please stay.

(He withdraws.)

VIOLETTA
Amor dunque non più.
Vi garba il patto?

VIOLETTA
Then - no more love.
Do you accept the pact?

ALFREDO
Io v'obbedisco. Parto.

ALFREDO
I obey. I shall leave you.

VIOLETTA *(si toglie un fiore dal seno)*
A tal giungeste?
Prendete questo fiore.

VIOLETTA *(taking a flower from her bosom)*
It's like that, then?
Take this flower.

ALFREDO
Perché?

ALFREDO
Why?

VIOLETTA
Per riportarlo -

ALFREDO
Quando?

VIOLETTA
Quando sarà appassito.

ALFREDO
Oh! Ciel! Domani -

VIOLETTA
Ebben, domani.

ALFREDO *(prende con trasporto il fiore)*
Io son felice!

VIOLETTA
D'amarmi dite ancora?

ALFREDO *(per partire)*
Oh, quanto v'amo!

VIOLETTA
Partite?

ALFREDO *(torna a lei, le bacia la mano)*
Parto.

VIOLETTA
Addio.

ALFREDO
Di più non bramo.

VIOLETTA
You shall bring it back -

ALFREDO
When?

VIOLETTA
When it has withered.

ALFREDO
Oh Heavens! Tomorrow.

VIOLETTA
Good, tomorrow.

ALFREDO *(joyously accepting the flower)*
I am happy!

VIOLETTA
Do you still think you love me?

ALFREDO *(about to leave)*
Oh, how much I love you!

VIOLETTA
You are leaving?

ALFREDO *(coming near her, kissing her hand)*
I am leaving.

VIOLETTA
Goodbye.

ALFREDO
I desire nothing more.

ALFREDO, VIOLETTA
Addio. Addio.

ALFREDO, VIOLETTA
Goodbye. Goodbye.

(Alfredo goes out as the other guests return to the drawing room, flushed from dancing.)

DISC NO.1/TRACK 7

The exhilarating gaiety of the guests's music as they take their leave of Violetta reflects the exhausting relentlessness of the pleasure-seekers's lifestyle.

TUTTI
Si ridesta in ciel l'aurora
e n'è forza di partire;
mercé a voi, gentil signora,
di sì splendido gioir.
La città di feste è piena,
volge il tempo dei piacer;
nel riposo ancor la lena
si ritempri per goder.

ALL
Dawn is breaking in the sky
and we must leave.
Thank you, gentle lady,
for this delightful evening.
The city is filled with parties,
the season of pleasure is at its height.
We shall sleep now, to regain our strength
for another night of joy.

(They go out.)

DISC NO.1/TRACK 8

Alone, Violetta muses on Alfredo's expressions of love. This begins a scene lasting twelve and a half minutes—a real tour de force for the solo soprano on stage.

VIOLETTA *(sola)*
È strano! È strano! In core
scolpiti ho quegli accenti!
Saria per me sventura un serio amore?
Che risolvi, o turbata anima mia?

VIOLETTA *(alone)*
How strange! How strange! His words
are burned upon my heart!
Would a real love be a tragedy for me?
What decision are you taking, oh my soul?

A dress rehearsal at the Glyndebourne Festival Opera

Null'uomo ancora t'accendeva - O gioia	No man has ever made me fall in love.
ch'io non conobbi, esser amata amando!	What joy, such as I have never known -
E sdegnarla poss'io	loving, being loved!
per l'aride follie del viver mio?	And can I scorn it
	for the arid nonsense of my present life?

Ah, fors'è lui, is a very well-known and masterfully constructed aria. It begins with halting phrases in a minor key as Violetta reflects on her strange reaction to Alfredo's declaration of love. The moment is truly internal, and the music requires a thoroughly different vocal expression than anything Violetta has yet sung. Her reflections eventually include the great love theme Alfredo had sung, sounding here almost like a prayer.

Ah, fors'è lui che l'anima	Ah, perhaps he is the one
solinga ne' tumulti	whom my soul,
godea sovente pingere	lonely in the tumult, loved
de' suoi colori occulti!	to imagine in secrecy!
Lui che modesto e vigile	Watchful though I never knew it,
all'egre soglie ascese,	he came here while I lay sick,
e nuova febbre accese,	awakening a new fever,
destandomi all'amor.	the fever of love,
A quell'amor ch'è palpito	of love which is the very breath
dell'universo intero,	of the universe itself -
misterioso, altero,	Mysterious and noble,
croce e delizia al cor!	both cross and ecstasy of the heart.

Follie! Follie! In a sudden change of mood, Violetta escapes her reverie and reasserts her preference for her gay lifestyle. The orchestra skips along with her as what is mainly a role for lyric soprano becomes a coloratura showpiece.

Follie! follie! Delirio vano è questo!	Folly! All is folly! This is mad delirium!
Povera donna, sola,	A poor woman, alone, lost in this

abbandonata in questo
popoloso deserto
che appellano Parigi. Che spero or più?
Che far degg'io? Gioire,
di voluttà ne' vortici perir.
Gioir, gioir!

crowded desert which is known to men as
Paris. What can I hope for?
What should I do? Revel
in the whirlpool of earthly pleasures.
Revel in joy! Ah!

DISC NO.1/TRACK 11

Sempre libera ("Forever free"). Violetta defines her creed in this most famous and difficult cabaletta. (The term is derived from the Italian word, cavallo, meaning "horse," and
the music gallops along appropriately.) In an interesting dramatic effect, Alfredo's voice
is heard from outside, declaring again his love for her (00:59), but Violetta will not be
swayed. Her declaration of independence brings the act to a close with a stunning penul-
timate E-flat above high C—a note not written by Verdi, but a modern embellishment
expected by most modern listeners.

Sempre libera degg'io
folleggiare di gioia in gioia,
vo' che scorra il viver mio
pei sentieri del piacer.
Nasca il giorno, o il giorno muoia,
sempre lieta ne' ritrovi,
a diletti sempre nuovi
dee volare il mio pensier.

Forever free, I must pass
madly from joy to joy.
My life's course shall be
forever in the paths of pleasure.
Whether it be dawn or dusk,
I must always live. Ah!
Gaily in the world's gay places,
ever seeking newer joys.

ALFREDO (*sotto al balcone*)
Amore, amor è palpito...

ALFREDO (*outdoors, under the balcony*)
Love is the very breath...

VIOLETTA
Oh!

VIOLETTA
Oh!

ALFREDO
...dell'universo intero -

ALFREDO
...of the universe itself -

VIOLETTA

Oh amore.

ALFREDO

Misterioso, misterioso, altero,
croce, croce e delizia,
croce e delizia, delizia al cor.

VIOLETTA

Follie! follie! Ah sì! Gioir, gioir!
Sempre libera degg'io
folleggiare di gioia in gioia,
vo' che scorra il viver mio
pei sentieri del piacer.
Nasca il giorno, o il giorno muoia,
sempre lieta ne' ritrovi,
a diletti sempre nuovi,
dee volare il mio pensier.

ALFREDO

Amor è palpito
dell'universo -

VIOLETTA

Ah! Dee volar il mio pensier.
Ah! il mio pensier. Il mio pensier.

VIOLETTA

Love.

ALFREDO

Mysterious and noble,
both cross and ecstasy,
cross and ecstasy of the heart.

VIOLETTA

Folly! Folly! Ah yes! From joy to joy,
forever free, I must pass
madly from joy to joy.
My life's course shall be
forever in the paths of pleasure.
Whether it be dawn or dusk,
I must always live. Ah!
Gaily in the world's gay places,
ever seeking newer joys, etc.

ALFREDO

Love is the very breath
of the universe itself.

VIOLETTA

Oh! My thoughts have to seek new joys.
Oh! My thoughts. My thoughts.

Act 2

SCENE ONE

A country house near Paris. A drawing room on the ground floor. In the background, facing the audience, there is a fireplace; on the mantelpiece, a clock and above it a mirror. On either side of the fireplace, French doors open on a garden. On the floor above, two other doors, facing each other. Chairs, tables, books, writing materials.

(Alfredo enters in hunting clothes.)

DISC NO. 1/TRACK 12

The second act begins in the idyllic setting of Alfredo and Violetta's country hideaway. The vigorous introduction in the strings describes the joy of the young lovers in their new life together.

DISC NO. 1/TRACK 13

De' miei bollenti spiriti is another famous aria which frequently finds its way to the concert stage. Accompanied by energetic pizzicato strings, Alfredo pours out his youthful, ardent euphoria. Verdi did not specify a tempo for this aria, and interpretations vary widely. It is sometimes performed very quickly, emphasizing Alfredo's impetuosity. In this performance, a statelier rendition convinces us of the sincerity of Alfredo's love.

ALFREDO *(depone il fucile)*
Lunge da lei per me non v'ha diletto!
Volaron già tre lune
dacché la mia Violetta
agi per me lasciò, dovizie, amori
e le pompose feste ov'agli omaggi avvezza,
vedea schiavo ciascun di sua bellezza.

ALFREDO *(putting down his shotgun)*
I have no joy in life when she is far away!
Three months have passed
since Violetta gave up for me
a life of ease, luxury, love affairs
and the pomp of society, where, surrounded
by adoration, she enslaved all with her

Ed or contenta in questi ameni luoghi
tutto scorda per me. Qui presso
a lei io rinascer mi sento.
E dal soffio d'amor rigenerato
scordo ne' gaudi suoi tutto il passato.
De' miei bollenti spiriti
il giovanile ardore
ella temprò col placido sorriso dell'amor!
Dal dì che disse: Vivere
io voglio a te fedel, ah, sì
dell'universo immemore,
io vivo quasi in ciel.

beauty. Now, happy in this quiet country
home, she has forgotten everything for me.
And here, near her, I feel like a man
reborn; invigorated by the pulse of love,
I have forgotten the past in the joy of being
with her. The violent fire of my youthful
spirits was tempered by the quiet smile of
her love!
Ever since the day when she said:
"I want to live only for you"
I seem to live in heaven,
unmindful of the world.

(Annina enters, dressed for travelling.)

DISC NO.1/TRACK 14

As Alfredo grills Annina regarding the reasons for her trip to Paris, he is accompanied by agitated figures in the strings. However sincere Alfredo may be in his love, he is still insecure about the relationship.

ALFREDO
Annina, donde vieni?

ALFREDO
Annina, where have you come from?

ANNINA
Da Parigi.

ANNINA
From Paris.

ALFREDO
Chi tel commise?

ALFREDO
Who sent you?

ANNINA
Fu la mia signora.

ANNINA
My mistress.

ALFREDO
Perché?

ALFREDO
Why?

ANNINA

Per alienar cavalli, cocchi,
e quanto ancor possiede.

ALFREDO

Che mai sento!

ANNINA

Lo spendio è grande a viver qui solinghi.

ALFREDO

E tacevi?

ANNINA

Mi fu il silenzio imposto.

ALFREDO

Imposto? Or v'abbisogna?

ANNINA

Mille luigi.

ALFREDO

Or vanne - andrò a Parigi.
Questo colloquio non sappia la signora.
Il tutto valgo a riparare ancora.

ANNINA

To take the horses, the carriages,
and whatever else is hers.

ALFREDO

What is this!

ANNINA

It is very expensive, living here all alone.

ALFREDO

What are you hiding from me?

ANNINA

I was sworn to silence.

ALFREDO

Sworn! Tell me, how much is needed?

ANNINA

A thousand louis.

ALFREDO

Go now - I shall go to Paris.
Madam must know nothing of our talk.
I can still take care of everything.

DISC NO. 1/TRACK 15

This piece is a cabaletta for tenor, frequently cut by at least half, if not altogether, because it tends to hold up the dramatic action. In this recording, it is restored in full and ends on a magnificent high C!

Oh mio rimorso! Oh, infamia!
Io vissi in tale errore.

Oh remorse! Oh infamy!
I have lived in such blind ignorance.

Ma il turpe sonno a frangere,	But this vile torpor has been broken,
Il ver mi balenò!	By the flash of truth!
Per poco in seno acquetaiti,	Lie pacified for a brief time in my breast,
O grido dell'onore;	Oh, cry of honor;
M'avrai securo vindice;	You will have sure vengeance of me;
Quest'onta laverò.	I will wash away this shame.
O mio rossor! Oh infamia!	Oh shame! Oh infamy!
Ah si, quest'onta laverò, *ecc.*	Oh yes, I will wash away this shame, *etc.*
O mio rossor! Oh infamia! *ecc.*	Oh remorse! O infamy! *etc.*

(He leaves. Soon Violetta enters with various papers in her hand. She speaks with Annina.)

DISC NO. 1/TRACK 16

Alfredo's father enters the scene to an ominous theme in the low strings [1:04]. Thus begins the long confrontation scene between Germont and Violetta, in many ways the emotional core of the whole opera. The music will shift at several points as the two negotiate their various claims.

VIOLETTA	**VIOLETTA**
Alfredo?	Alfredo?
ANNINA	**ANNINA**
Per Parigi or or partiva.	He has just left for Paris.
VIOLETTA	**VIOLETTA**
E tornerà?	When will he come back?
ANNINA	**ANNINA**
Pria che tramonti il giorno -	Before evening.
dirvel m'impose -	He asked me to tell you.
VIOLETTA	**VIOLETTA**
È strano!	How strange!
ANNINA *(presentandole una lettera)*	**ANNINA** *(handing her a letter)*
Per voi.	For you.

VIOLETTA *(prendendola)*
Sta ben. In breve
giungerà un uom d'affari -
entri all'istante.

(Violetta, reading the letter)

Ah, ah! Scopriva Flora il mio ritiro.
E m'invita a danzar per questa sera!
Invan m'aspetterà.

ANNINA
È qui un signore.

VIOLETTA
Sarà lui che attendo.

(She gestures for Annina to admit him. Giorgio Germont enters.)

GERMONT
Madamigella Valéry?

VIOLETTA
Son io.

GERMONT
D'Alfredo il padre in me vedete!

VIOLETTA

(Surprised, she offers him a chair.)

Voi!

VIOLETTA *(taking it)*
Good. In a few minutes a man is coming
on business.
Show him in immediately.

Aha! Flora has found my hideaway! She has
invited me to a dance this evening!
She'll wait for me in vain.

ANNINA
A gentleman to see you.

VIOLETTA
It must be the man I'm expecting.

GERMONT
Mademoiselle Valéry?

VIOLETTA
Yes.

GERMONT
I am Alfredo's father!

VIOLETTA

You!

Alfredo (Walter MacNeil), distraught over Violetta's sudden departure

GERMONT
Sì, dell'incauto, che a ruina corre,
ammaliato da voi.

VIOLETTA *(risentita, alzandosi)*
Donna son io, signore, ed in mia casa;
ch'io vi lasci assentite
più per voi che per me.

(She is on the point of going out.)

GERMONT
(Quai modi!) Pure -

VIOLETTA
Tratto in error voi foste.

GERMONT
De' suoi beni egli dono vuol farvi.

VIOLETTA
Non l'osò finora - rifiuterei.

GERMONT *(guardando intorno)*
Pur tanto lusso -

VIOLETTA
A tutti è mistero quest'atto.
A voi nol sia.

(She gives him the paper.)

GERMONT *(Germont scorre le carte.)*
Ciel! Che discopro!
D'ogni vostro avere or volete spogliarvi?
Ah, il passato, perché v'accusa?

GERMONT
Yes, father of this reckless lad, who is
rushing to his ruin because of you.

VIOLETTA *(rising, with resentment)*
I, sir, am a woman and in my own home.
Now please excuse me,
more for your sake than for mine.

GERMONT
(What spirit!) And yet -

VIOLETTA
You have been badly advised.

GERMONT
He wants to give you all his possessions.

VIOLETTA
So far, he hasn't dared - I should refuse.

GERMONT *(looking about him)*
Such luxury -

VIOLETTA
This paper is a secret from everyone.
But it shall not be from you.

GERMONT *(after looking at them briefly)*
Heavens! What is this!
You wish to sell everything you own?
Ah, why does your past accuse you so?

VIOLETTA

Più non esiste - or amo Alfredo, e Dio
lo cancellò col pentimento mio.

VIOLETTA

The past does not exist - I love Alfredo
now; God wiped out my past with my
repentance.

GERMONT

Nobili sensi invero!

GERMONT

These are truly noble sentiments!

VIOLETTA

Oh, come dolce mi suona il vostro accento!

VIOLETTA

Ah, how good to hear these words from you!

GERMONT

Ed a tai sensi
un sacrifizio chieggo -

GERMONT

And in the name of these sentiments, I ask
a sacrifice -

VIOLETTA *(alzandosi)*

Ah, no, tacete - terribil cosa chiedereste
certo.Il previdi - v'attesi - era
felice troppo.

VIOLETTA *(arising)*

Ah, no, do not say it. Certainly you would
ask some frightening thing. I knew it - I
expected you - I was too happy.

GERMONT

D'Alfredo il padre
la sorte, l'avvenir domanda or qui
de' suoi due figli.

GERMONT

Alfredo's father
asks you to decide the fate
of his two children.

VIOLETTA

Di due figli!

VIOLETTA

His two children!

DISC NO. 1/TRACK 17

Germont begins his entreaty lyrically as he tries to coax Violetta into pitying the difficult
position of his lovely and innocent daughter.

GERMONT

Sì!
Pura siccome un angelo

GERMONT

Yes.
God blessed me with a daughter,

Iddio mi diè una figlia;
se Alfredo nega riedere
in seno alla famiglia,
l'amato e amante giovine
cui sposa andar dovea,
or si ricusa al vincolo
che lieti ne rendeva.
Deh, non mutate in triboli
le rose dell'amor.
A' prieghi miei resistere no, no
non voglia il vostro cor.

VIOLETTA
Ah, comprendo - dovrò per alcun tempo
da Alfredo allontanarmi - doloroso
fora per me - pur -

GERMONT
Non è ciò che chiedo.

VIOLETTA
Cielo, che più cercate?
Offersi assai!

GERMONT
Pur non basta.

VIOLETTA
Volete che per sempre a lui rinunzi?

GERMONT
È d'uopo!

like an angel in her purity;
if Alfredo refuses to return
to the bosom of his family,
the young man in love and beloved in turn,
who was soon to marry my daughter,
would reject this bond
on which our happiness depends.
Ah, do not be the cause of love's roses
changing into thorns.
Do not let your heart refuse
what I so fervently ask of you. No! No!

VIOLETTA
Ah, I understand - I must leave Alfredo
for a time. It will be painful
for me - yet -

GERMONT
That is not what I ask.

VIOLETTA
Heaven, what more can you ask!
I offered much!

GERMONT
But not enough.

VIOLETTA
You want me to give him up forever?

GERMONT
You must!

Violett's phrases become breathy as she begins to realize the exorbitant price of Germont's request.

VIOLETTA	**VIOLETTA**
Ah no! - giammai! No, no!	No - never! No, no!
Non sapete quale affetto	Can you not see what tremendous,
vivo, immenso m'arda in petto?	burning love I feel for him,
Che né amici, né parenti	I, who have no friends or family
io non conto tra' viventi?	among the living?
E che Alfredo m'ha giurato	Don't you know that Alfredo swore
che in lui tutto troverò?	that I should find everything in him?
Non sapete che colpita	Don't you know that my life
d'atro morbo è la mia vita?	is endangered by a terrible disease,
Che già presso il fine vedo?	that I have but a short time to live?
Ch'io mi separi da Alfredo!	To leave Alfredo forever?
Ah, il supplizio è sì spietato,	Ah, the anguish would be so cruel
che a morir preferirò.	that I should prefer to die.
GERMONT	**GERMONT**
È grave il sacrifizio,	The sacrifice is great,
ma pur tranquilla uditemi,	but hear me out patiently.
bella voi siete e giovine -	You are still young and beautiful -
col tempo -	in time -
VIOLETTA	**VIOLETTA**
Ah, più non dite -	Ah, say nothing more.
v'intendo - m'è impossibile.	I understand - I cannot -
Lui solo amar vogl'io.	I shall never love anyone but him.
GERMONT	**GERMONT**
Sia pure - ma volubile sovente è l'uom -	That may well be - but men are often fickle.
VIOLETTA	**VIOLETTA**
Gran Dio!	Oh God!

Germont tries a new tack with Violetta, focusing on the fickle nature of men and playing on Violetta's fears of aging. His music becomes extremely sinister and manipulative.

GERMONT

Un dì, quando le veneri
il tempo avra fugate,
fia presto il tedio a sorgere -
che sarà allor? Pensate -
per voi non avran balsamo
i più soavi affetti,
poiché dal ciel non furono
tai nodi benedetti.

GERMONT

Once time has staled
the delights of love,
tedium will follow quickly.
Then what? Think -
Even the deepest feelings
can bring you no balm,
since this bond was never
blessed by heaven.

VIOLETTA

È vero! È vero!

VIOLETTA

It's true! It's true!

GERMONT

Ah, dunque sperdasi tal sogno seduttore.

GERMONT

Ah, then lay aside this beguiling dream.

VIOLETTA

È vero! È vero!

VIOLETTA

It's true! It's true!

GERMONT

Siate di mia famiglia l'angel consolatore
Violetta, deh, pensateci, ne siete in tempo
ancor. È Dio che ispira, o giovine,
tai detti a un genitor.

GERMONT

Be rather the consoling angel
of my family. Violetta. Think -
You still have time. Young lady, it is God
who inspires these words on a father's lips.

VIOLETTA

Così alla misera ch'è un dì caduta,
di più risorgere speranza è muta!
Se pur benefico le indulga Iddio,
l'uomo implacabil per lei sarà.

VIOLETTA

All hope of rising again is forever gone.
For the wretched woman who erred one
day! Even if God grants her mercy
charitably Man will always be implacable.

GERMONT

Siate di mia famiglia l'angiol consolator.

GERMONT

Be rather the consoling angel of my family.

VIOLETTA *(poi, piangendo, a Germont)*

Ah! dite alla giovine sì bella e pura
ch'avvi una vittima della sventura,
cui resta un unico raggio di bene -
che a lei il sacrifica e che morrà!

VIOLETTA *(then, to Germont as she weeps)*

Oh, tell your daughter, so lovely and pure,
that a poor and wretched woman,
who has but one precious thing in life -
will sacrifice it for her - and then will die!

GERMONT

Piangi, piangi, o misera, supremo, il veggo,
è il sacrifizio che ora ti chieggo.
Sento nell'anima già le tue pene;
coraggio e il nobile tuo cor vincerà!

GERMONT

Weep, weep, poor girl. I see now
that the sacrifice I asked could not be
greater. Within my heart I feel what you
must suffer; be brave, your noble heart will
conquer all.

DISC 1/TRACK 20

Violetta's response is in hushed phrases in the haunting key of E flat, suggesting someone who is physically stunned and summoning all her strength to suppress her true emotions. Germont's interjections are sympathetic yet still stern and not consoling.

VIOLETTA

Dite alla giovine sì bella e pura
ch'avvi una vittima della sventura,
cui resta un unico raggio di bene
che a lei il sacrifica e che morrà!

VIOLETTA

Tell your daughter, so lovely and pure,
that a poor and wretched woman,
who has but one precious thing in life -
will sacrifice it for her - and then will die!

GERMONT

Ah supremo, il veggo,
è il sacrificio ch'ora ti chieggo.
Sento nell'anima già le tue pene;
coraggio e il nobile cor vincerà!
Piangi, o misera!

GERMONT

I see now that the sacrifice I asked could,
not be greater, within my heart I feel what
you must suffer, be brave, your noble heart
will conquer all.
Weep, poor girl.

A very quiet tone pervades as Violetta and Germont dare not say that she must tell Alfredo she has left him for another man. The tension, and emotion, builds in the orchestra here, rather than the vocal lines.

VIOLETTA
Imponete.

VIOLETTA
Tell me what I must do.

GERMONT
Non amarlo ditegli.

GERMONT
Tell him you don't love him.

VIOLETTA
Nol crederà.

VIOLETTA
He won't believe me.

GERMONT
Partite.

GERMONT
Go away, then.

VIOLETTA
Seguirammi.

VIOLETTA
He will follow me.

GERMONT
Allor -

GERMONT
Then -

VIOLETTA
Qual figlia m'abbracciate,
forte così sarò.

VIOLETTA
Embrace me as if I were your daughter -
it will give me strength.

(They embrace.)

Tra breve ei vi fia reso.
Ma afflitto oltre ogni dire.

Soon he will be yours again,
but desperately sad.

(pointing to the garden)

A suo conforto di colà volerete.

Out there you will hurry to comfort him.

(Violetta sits down to write.)

GERMONT	**GERMONT**
Che pensate?	What is it?

VIOLETTA	**VIOLETTA**
Sapendo, v'opporreste al pensier mio.	If I told you, you would oppose my wish.

GERMONT	**GERMONT**
Generosa! E per voi che far poss'io?	Generous woman! What can I do for you?
O generosa!	Generous woman!

DISC NO. 1/TRACK 22

Emotions finally burst forth in this section, as Germont tries to encourage Violetta in music reminiscent of people preparing for war. They then exchange sympathetic farewells.

VIOLETTA *(tornando a lui)*	**VIOLETTA** *(returning near him)*
Morrò! La mia memoria non fia ch'ei	I shall die! Let him not curse my memory;
maledica, se le mie pene orribili vi sia chi	when I am dead, let someone tell him of
almen gli dica.	my suffering.

GERMONT	**GERMONT**
No, generosa, vivere,	No, generous woman, you must live,
e lieta voi dovrete;	and live in happiness.
mercè di queste lagrime	Heaven one day will recompense these
dal cielo un giorno avrete.	tears.

VIOLETTA	**VIOLETTA**
Conosca il sacrifizio	Let him know the sacrifice
ch'io consumai d'amore -	which I made for love -
che sarà suo fin l'ultimo	for the very last breath of life
sospiro del mio cor.	will be for him alone.

GERMONT

Premiato il sacrifizio
sarà del vostro core;
d'un'opra così nobile
sarete fiera allor. Sì, sì

VIOLETTA

Conosca il sacrifizio
ch'io consumai d'amore -
che sarà suo fin l'ultimo
sospiro del mio cor.

GERMONT

Sarete fiera allor.
D'un'opra così nobile
sarete fiera allor.
Premiato il sacrifizio
sarà del vostro cor;
d'un'opra così nobil
sarete fiera allor.

VIOLETTA

Qui giunge alcun! Partite!

GERMONT

Oh, grato v'è il cor mio!

VIOLETTA

Partite! Non ci vedrem più forse

(They embrace.)

VIOLETTA, GERMONT

Siate felice!

GERMONT

And your heart's sacrifice
will be rewarded.
Then your heart will be proud
of so noble an act. Yes, yes, yes -

VIOLETTA

Let him know the sacrifice
which I made for love -
For the very last breath of life
will be for him alone.

GERMONT

Of so noble an act
then your heart will be proud
of so noble an act.
And your heart's sacrifice
will be rewarded.
Then your heart will be proud
of so noble an act.

VIOLETTA

Someone is coming…you must leave.

GERMONT

Oh, how grateful I am to you!

VIOLETTA

Leave me. We may never see each other
again.

VIOLETTA, GERMONT

May you be happy.

VIOLETTA	VIOLETTA
Addio!	Goodbye!

GERMONT	GERMONT
Addio!	Goodbye!

VIOLETTA	VIOLETTA
Conosca il sacrifizio,	Let him know the sacrifice…

GERMONT	GERMONT
Sì!	Yes.

VIOLETTA	VIOLETTA
…ch'io consumai d'amore -	…which I made for love…
che sarà suo fin l'ultimo…	…for the very last breath of life.
Addio!	Goodbye!

GERMONT	GERMONT
Addio!	Goodbye!

VIOLETTA	VIOLETTA
che sarà suo fin l'ultimo…	…for the very last breath of life.
Addio!	Goodbye!

VIOLETTA, GERMONT	VIOLETTA, GERMONT
Felice siate, addio!	May you be happy…goodbye!

(Germont goes out through the garden door.)

DISC NO. 1/TRACK 23
Violetta says little while writing Alfredo, and a plaintive clarinet gives voice to her sighs.

VIOLETTA	VIOLETTA
Dammi tu forza, o cielo!	Give me strength, oh Heaven!

(She sits down and writes, then rings for the servant...Annina enters.)

ANNINA
Mi richiedeste?

ANNINA
You rang for me?

VIOLETTA
Sì, reca tu stessa questo foglio.

VIOLETTA
Yes, please deliver this letter yourself.

(Annina reads the address, then looks up in surprise.)

Silenzio - va' all'istante.

Silence - go immediately.

(Annina goes out.)

Ed or si scriva a lui.
Che gli dirò? Chi men darà il coraggio?

And now to write to him.
What can I say? Who will give me courage?

(She writes, then seals the letter.)

DISC NO. 1/TRACK 24

Alfredo enters, and over an agitated figure in the orchestra, he questions Violetta about the letter. The tension continues (00:40) as she asks him to meet his father after she has gone. At the piece's climax (01:40), we hear the expansive theme we heard in the Prelude over tremolo strings. Here, the theme is all raw emotion and a great demand on the lyric soprano, but crucial for the convincing expression of her love.

ALFREDO *(Entra.)*
Che fai?

ALFREDO *(entering)*
What are you doing?

VIOLETTA

VIOLETTA

(concealing the letter)

Nulla.

Nothing.

ALFREDO
Scrivevi?

VIOLETTA
Sì - no

ALFREDO
Qual turbamento! A chi scrivevi?

VIOLETTA
A te -

ALFREDO
Dammi quel foglio.

VIOLETTA
No, per ora.

ALFREDO
Mi perdona - son io preoccupato -

VIOLETTA
Che fu?

ALFREDO
Giunse mio padre -

VIOLETTA
Lo vedesti?

ALFREDO
Ah, no: severo scritto mi lasciava.
Però l'attendo, t'amerà in vederti.

ALFREDO
You were writing?

VIOLETTA
Yes - no -

ALFREDO
But what confusion! To whom were you writing?

VIOLETTA
To you -

ALFREDO
Give me the letter.

VIOLETTA
No, not now.

ALFREDO
Forgive me - I am concerned about -

VIOLETTA
What has happened?

ALFREDO
My father was here.

VIOLETTA
Did you see him?

ALFREDO
Ah, no. He left a stern letter for me.
But I'm expecting him. He'll love you at first sight.

VIOLETTA

Ch'ei qui non mi sorprenda,
lascia che m'allontani - tu lo calma -
ai piedi suoi mi getterò -
divisi ei più non ne vorrà -
sarem felici -
perché tu m'ami, Alfredo, non è vero?

ALFREDO

Oh, quanto! Perché piangi?

VIOLETTA

Di lagrime aveva d'uopo -
or son tranquilla -
lo vedi? Ti sorrido - lo vedi?
Sarò là tra quei fior presso a te sempre.
Amami, Alfredo, quant'io t'amo.
Addio!

VIOLETTA

He must not find me here.
Let me go away - you calm him -
I'll throw myself at his feet - then
he'll not want to separate us. We shall be
happy - because you love me, you love me
Alfredo, you love me, don't you?

ALFREDO

So much! Why are you weeping?

VIOLETTA

I needed tears -
now I feel better -
See? I am smiling at you - see?
I shall always be here, near you, among the
flowers.
Love me, Alfredo, love me as much as I
love you.
Goodbye!

(She runs out into the garden.)

DISC NO. 2/TRACK 1

Alfredo's fears are so persistent that he only reads the first few words of Violetta's letter before he breaks down.

ALFREDO

Ah, vive sol quel core all'amor mio!

ALFREDO

Ah, this dear one lives only for my love!

(He sits down, reads a book for a moment. Then he stands up and goes to look at the clock on the mantel.)

È tardi; ed oggi forse
più non verrà mio padre.

It is late: perhaps today
my father will not come.

(Alfredo's father is seen at a distance, crossing the garden.)

Qualcuno è nel giardino!	Someone is in the garden!
Chi è là?	Who is it?

(He is on the point of going out.)

COMMISSIONARIO
Il signor Germont?

MESSENGER
Signor Germont?

ALFREDO
Son io.

ALFREDO
I am he.

COMMISSIONARIO
Una dama
da un cocchio, per voi, di qua non lunge,
mi diede questo scritto.

MESSENGER
A lady in a carriage, not far down the road,
gave me this letter.

(He gives the letter to Alfredo, who tips him.)

ALFREDO
Di Violetta! Perché son io commosso!
A raggiungerla forse ella m'invita -
Io tremo! Oh ciel! Coraggio!

ALFREDO
From Violetta! Why am I so upset?
Perhaps she wants me to join her -
I am trembling. Oh, Heaven! Courage!

(He opens the letter and reads:)

"Alfredo, al giungervi di questo foglio…"

"Alfredo, by the time you receive this letter"

(thunderstruck, he cries out:)

Ah!

Ah!

(Turning, he sees his father, and throws himself into his arms.)

Padre mio!

Father!

GERMONT

Mio figlio!

Oh, quanto soffri! Oh, tergi il pianto -

ritorna di tuo padre orgoglio e vanto.

GERMONT

My son!

Oh, how you are suffering!

Ah, dry your tears - be once again your

father's pride.

(In despair, Alfredo sits down at the table, his head in his hands.)

DISC NO. 2/TRACK 2

Di Provenza il mar il suol is one of the most outstanding baritone arias in the repertoire.
The opening theme, played by woodwinds in thirds, has a folk-like quality which describes
the rural setting that was Alfredo's childhood home. The aria has the structure of music
written a generation before Verdi, and therefore is appropriate to represent the point of
view of the older generation as well as having an inherently old-fashioned feel.

Di Provenza il mar, il suol

chi dal cor ti cancellò?

Chi dal cor i cancellò, di Provenza

il mar, il suol?

Al natio fulgente sol qual destino ti furò?

Qual destino ti furò al natio fulgene sol?

Oh, rammenta pur nel duol

ch'ivi gioia a te brillò;

E che pace colà sol su te splendere ancor può.

Dio mi guidò!

Ah! il tuo vecchio genitor

tu non sai quanto soffrì.

Te lontano, di squallor

il suo tetto si coprì.

Il suo tetto si coprì di squallore, di squallor,

Ma se alfin ti trovo ancor,

se in me speme non fallì,

se la voce dell'onor

in te appien non ammutì,

The sea, the hills of Provence,

who effaced them from your heart?

Who has erased the memory from

your heart?

What destiny took you away

from the sunny land of your birth?

Oh, what destiny drove you away?

Oh, remember in your sorrow

what joy warmed you there;

and that only there can your soul find

peace again.

God brought me here!

Ah! You cannot know how your old father

has suffered.

With you away his house is clouded with

sorrow. In deepest sadness his roof has been

shrouded.

But if at last I have found you,

if my hope has not been in vain.

Ma se alfin ti trovo ancor, *ecc.*	If the voice of honour is not wholly stilled
Dio m'esaudì! *ecc.*	in you. But I have found you again, *etc.*
	God has answered my prayer! *etc.*

(embracing him)

| Nè rispondi d'un padre all'affetto? | Don't you return your father's love? |

DISC NO. 2/TRACKS 3 & 4

No, non udrai rimproveri begins as a stately cabaletta as Germont continues to persuade
his son to abandon his love nest. Tension builds (01:54) as he is interrupted by Alfredo,
who hasn't heard a word. The scene crashes to a dramatic close (03:24) as Alfredo storms
from the house, seeking revenge for his lost love. This exciting aria is rarely heard in
live performance.

ALFREDO

Mille serpi divoranmi il petto.

Mi lasciate.

ALFREDO

A thousand furies are torturing my breast.

Leave me.

GERMONT

Lasciarti!

GERMONT

Leave you!

ALFREDO

ALFREDO

(resolute)

(Oh vendetta!)

(Oh, revenge!)

GERMONT

Non più indugi; partiamo – t'affretta –

GERMONT

Do not delay; let us go – be quick –

ALFREDO

(Ah, fu Douphol!)

ALFREDO

(Ah, it was Douphol!)

GERMONT

M'ascolti tu?

ALFREDO

No!

GERMONT

Dunque invano trovato t'avrò.
No, non udrai rimproveri;
Copriam d'oblio il passato;
L'amor che m'ha guidato
Sa tutto perdonar.
Vieni, i tuoi in giubilo,
Con me rivedi ancora
A chi penò fnora
Tal gioia non negar.
Un padre ed una suora –
T'affretta a consolare.
No, non udrai rimproveri, *ecc.*

ALFREDO

Mille serpi divranmi il petto...

GERMONT

M'ascolti tu?

ALFREDO

No!

GERMONT

Un padre ed una suora -
T'affretta a consolar.
No, non udrai rimroveri, *ecc.*

GERMONT

Will you listen to me?

ALFREDO

No!

GERMONT

Then, have I found you in vain?
No, you shall hear no reproaches;
let us bury the past;
The love which guided me
Can pardon all.
Come, see your loved ones again,
Together with me.
Do not deny this happiness
To one who has suffered greatly.
Your father and your sister –
Hasten to console them.
No, you shall hear no reproaches, *etc.*

ALFREDO

A thousand furies are torturing my breast...

GERMONT

Are you listening?

ALFREDO

No!

GERMONT

Your father and your sister –
Hasten to console them.
No you shall hear no reproaches, *etc.*

ALFREDO	**ALFREDO**

ALFREDO

(Suddenly he sees Flora's letter on the table and exclaims:)

Ah! ell'è alla festa!	Ah! She is at the party! Let me fly
Volisi l'offesa a vendicar.	to take revenge for this offence.

GERMONT	**GERMONT**
Che dici! Ah, ferma!	What are you saying? Stop!

(Alfredo runs out of the house, followed by his father.)

SCENE TWO

A salon in Flora's home, richly furnished and brightly lighted. A door to the rear, others on either side. To the right, somewhat to the foreground, a gaming table with equipment for play; left, an elaborate table with flowers and refreshments; nearby, sofa and chairs.

(Flora, the Marquis and Dr. Grenvil enter with other guests - all chatting.)

DISC NO. 2/TRACK 5

In contrast to the drama of the previous scene, Verdi first treats us to the same type of party music we heard at the beginning of the opera.

FLORA	**FLORA**
Avrem lieta di maschere la notte:	Later we shall be entertained by masks:
n'è duce il viscontino -	the Viscount is in charge.
Violetta ed Alfredo anco invitai.	I've invited Violetta and Alfredo.

MARCHESE	**MARQUIS**
La novità ignorate?	Haven't you heard the news?
Violetta e Germont sono disgiunti.	Violetta and Germont have separated.

DOTTORE, FLORA	**DOCTOR, FLORA**
Fia vero?	Have they really?
MARCHESE	**MARQUIS**
Ella verrà qui col barone.	She is coming with the Baron.
DOTTORE	**DOCTOR**
Li vidi ieri ancor - parean felici.	I saw them only yesterday - they looked happy.

(The sound of laughing voices is heard.)

FLORA	**FLORA**
Silenzio - udite?	Silence - do you hear?
FLORA, DOTTORE, MARCHESE	**FLORA, DOCTOR, MARQUIS**
Giungono gli amici.	Our friends are coming.

DISC NO. 2/TRACK 6 & 7

Verdi interrupts the action with these Gypsy and Spanish entertainments. This lively music gives us a rest from the tension in the plot. Many of the ballets Verdi wrote for his other operas were later additions to existing scores, composed as concessions to local tastes in Paris where ballets in opera were de rigueur. Those are rarely performed within the operas today. This choral ballet, however, is always performed, since Verdi conceived it from the start as an important relief to the dramatic tension.

(Ladies disguised as gypsies enter.)

ZINGARE	**GYPSIES**
Noi siamo zingarelle	We are gypsies,
venute da lontano;	come from afar;
d'ognuno sulla mano	the fortunes of all
leggiamo l'avvenir.	we can read in their hands.
Se consultiam le stelle	When we call upon the stars,

null'avvi a noi d'oscuro,
e i casi del futuro
possiamo altrui predir.
Vediamo -

nothing is hidden from us,
and we can tell you all
what the future holds in store.
Let us see -

CORO I (*osservando la mano di Flora*)
Voi, signora, rivali alquante avete.

CHORUS I (*examining Flora's palm*)
You, Madam, have many rivals.

CORO II (*osservando la mano del Marchese*)
Marchese, voi non siete model di fedeltà.

CHORUS II (*examining the Marquis's palm*)
Marquis, you are scarcely a model of
fidelity.

FLORA (*al Marchese*)
Fate il galante ancora?
Ben, vo' me la paghiate -

FLORA (*to the Marquis*)
So you still play the gallant?
Fine - I'll make you pay for this.

MARCHESE
Che diamin vi pensate?
L'accusa è falsità.

MARQUIS
What the devil are you thinking?
It's a bare-faced lie.

FLORA
La volpe lascia il pelo,
non abbandona il vizio.
Marchese mio, giudizio,
o vi farò pentir.

FLORA
The fox may lose his brush,
but never abandons his rascality.
Take care, my dear Marquis,
or you'll be sorry, I swear.

TUTTI
Su via, si stenda un velo
sui fatti del passato;
già quel ch'è stato è stato,
badiamo/badate all'avvenir.

ALL
Come, come, whatever's happened
shall be veiled by the past;
what's been has been,
think only of what's to be.

(*Flora and the Marquis shake hands. Now from the right, Gastone and other men, dressed as Spanish matadors and picadors, enter.*)

GASTONE, MATTADORI

Di Madride noi siam mattadori,
siamo i prodi del circo dei tori,
testé giunti a godere del chiasso
che a Parigi si fa pel Bue grasso;
È una storia se udire vorrete,
quali amanti noi siamo saprete.

GLI ALTRI

Sì, sì, bravi; narrate, narrate:
con piacere l'udremo.

GASTONE, MATTADORI

Ascoltate.
È Piquillo un bel gagliardo
biscaglino mattador:
forte il braccio, fiero il guardo
delle giostre egli è signor.
D'Andalusa giovinetta
follemente innamorò;
ma la bella ritrosetta
così al giovane parlò:
"Cinque tori in un sol giorno
vo' vederti ad atterrar;
e, se vinci, al tuo ritorno
mano e cor ti vo' donar."
Sì, gli disse, e il mattadore,
alle giostre mosse il piè;
cinque tori, vincitore,
sull'arena egli stendé.

GLI ALTRI

Bravo, bravo il mattadore,
ben gagliardo si mostrò,
se alla giovane l'amore
in tal guisa egli provò!

GASTONE, MATADORS

We're matadors, from Madrid,
the champions of the bullring.
We've just arrived to join in the fun
of carnival time in Paris;
if you'll hear our story to the end,
you'll know what great lovers we are.

THE OTHERS

Yes, yes, good! Tell us, tell us:
we'll hear your story with pleasure.

GASTONE, MATADORS

Listen, then.
Piquillo is a strapping young man.
A matador from Biscay:
strong of arm and fierce of eye,
he is the lord of the bullring.
He fell for an Andalusian lass,
madly in love fell he;
but the stubborn little miss
answered him this way:
"Five bulls in a single day -
I'll see you kill them all;
and if you win, when you return,
my heart and hand are yours."
"Yes, yes." said he, and off he went,
to the bullring straight away;
five bulls our conquering hero met,
and killed them all that day.

THE OTHERS

Bravo, bravo, this matador -
he showed himself such a champion,
and, in so doing,
he proved his love!

GASTONE, MATTADORI	GASTONE AND MATADORS
Poi, tra plausi, ritornato	Then, amidst the applause,
alla bella del suo cor,	he went back to his love,
colse il premio desiato	and there received the longed-for prize,
tra le braccia dell'amor.	wrapped in his sweetheart's arms.

GLI ALTRI	THE OTHERS
Con tai prove i mattadori	It is with tests like this that matadors
san le belle conquistar!	sweep lovely women off their feet!

GASTONE, MATTADORI	GASTONE AND MATADORS
Ma qui son più miti i cori;	But here the thing is simpler;
a noi basta folleggiar.	it's enough for us if we can frolic.

TUTTI	ALL
Sì, allegri. Or pria tentiamo	Yes, with carefree gaiety. Now first
della sorte il vario umor;	let's try the humour of Fortune;
la palestra dischiudiamo	we'll open the ring
agli audaci giuocator.	to the dauntless gamblers.

(The men unmask. Some of them walk about, talking together, while the others prepare to play. Alfredo enters.)

DISC NO. 2/TRACK 8

Tension resumes as the card game begins (00:33), and the vocal lines take on a static quality with the exception of Violetta's asides (01:14, 02:26 and 03:20), which soar out over the texture expressing her distress.

TUTTI	ALL
Alfredo! Voi!	Alfredo! You!

ALFREDO	ALFREDO
Sì, amici -	Yes my friends -

FLORA
Violetta?

ALFREDO
Non ne so.

TUTTI
Ben disinvolto! Bravo!
Or via, giuocar si può.

(Gastone cuts the cards. Alfredo and others place their bets. Violetta enters, escorted by the Baron. Flora goes forward to meet her.)

FLORA
Qui desiata giungi.

VIOLETTA
Cessi al cortese invito.

FLORA
Grata vi son, barone, d'averlo pur gradito.

BARONE
Germont è qui! Il vedete?

VIOLETTA
Cielo! Gli è vero. Il vedo.

BARONE
Da voi non un sol detto
si volga a questo Alfredo -
non un detto, non un detto!

VIOLETTA
(Ah, perché venni, incauta!
Pietà, gran Dio, di me!)

FLORA
Violetta?

ALFREDO
I don't know where she is.

ALL
How nonchalant! Bravo!
Come, now we can play.

FLORA
I am so glad you have come.

VIOLETTA
I couldn't refuse your kind invitation.

FLORA
I am grateful to you, too, Baron, for coming.

BARON
Germont is here! Do you see him!

VIOLETTA
Heaven! It's true. I see him.

BARON
You will not say
one word to this Alfredo -
not one word, not one word!

VIOLETTA
(Ah, why was I so rash as to come!
Mercy, oh God!)

FLORA *(fa sedere Violetta presso di sé sul divano)*
Meco t'assidi; narrami -
quai novità vegg'io?

FLORA *(to Violetta, as she invites her to sit next to her on the sofa)*
Sit here with me, tell me - what is this I see?

(Dr. Grenvil approaches the two women, who are talking together in a low voice. The Marquis remains to one side with the Baron. Gastone deals the cards while Alfredo and various others bet. Still other guests are talking slowly here and there about the room.)

ALFREDO
Un quattro!

ALFREDO
A four!

GASTONE
Ancora hai vinto!

GASTONE
You win again!

ALFREDO
Sfortuna nell'amore fortuna reca al giuoco.

ALFREDO
Unlucky in love means luck at cards.

(He places his bet and wins again.)

TUTTI
È sempre vincitore!

ALL
He wins every time!

ALFREDO
Oh, vincerò stasera:
e l'oro guadagnato
poscia a goder
tra' campi ritornerò beato.

ALFREDO
Oh, tonight I shall win.
And with the gold
I shall return happily
to the country.

FLORA
Solo?

FLORA
Álone?

ALFREDO
No, no, con tale che vi fu meco ancora,
poi mi sfuggia -

ALFREDO
No, no, with one who was with me,
but ran away -

VIOLETTA
Mio Dio!

GASTONE

(to Alfredo, indicating Violetta)

Pietà di lei!

BARONE

(to Alfredo, making a bad job of restraining his anger)

Signor!

VIOLETTA *(al Barone)*
Frenatevi, o vi lascio.

ALFREDO
Barone, m'appellaste?

BARONE
Siete in sì gran fortuna,
che al giuoco mi tentaste.

ALFREDO *(ironico)*
Sì? La disfida accetto.

VIOLETTA
Che fia? Morir mi sento!
Pietà, gran Dio, di me!

BARONE *(punta)*
Cento luigi a destra.

VIOLETTA
Oh, God!

GASTONE

Take pity on her!

BARON

Sir!

VIOLETTA *(to the Baron)*
Restrain yourself, or I shall leave you.

ALFREDO
Baron, you called me?

BARON
Your luck is so good
I'm tempted to play.

ALFREDO *(ironically)*
Yes? I accept your challenge.

VIOLETTA
What will happen? I shall die!
Take pity, dear God, take pity on me!

BARON *(betting)*
A hundred louis on the right.

ALFREDO *(punta)*
Ed alla manca cento.

GASTONE
Un asso - un fante - hai vinto!

BARONE
Il doppio?

ALFREDO
Il doppio sia.

GASTONE *(tagliando)*
Un quattro, un sette.

TUTTI
Ancora!

ALFREDO
Pur la vittoria è mia!

CORO
Bravo davver!
La sorte è tutta per Alfredo!

FLORA
Del villeggiar la spesa
farà il baron, già il vedo.

ALFREDO
Seguite pur.

SERVO
La cena è pronta.

ALFREDO *(betting)*
On the left - a hundred.

GASTONE
Ace - jack - you win!

BARON
Double?

ALFREDO
Good - double.

GASTONE *(dealing)*
Four - seven.

ALL
Again!

ALFREDO
The victory is mine after all!

CHORUS
Bravo! Really,
luck is on Alfredo's side!

FLORA
The Baron has paid
for the holiday, I see.

ALFREDO
Continue if you wish.

A SERVANT
Dinner is served.

FLORA

Andiamo.

CORO (*Tutti partono.*)

Andiamo.

VIOLETTA

(*Che fia? morir mi sento!*
Pietà, gran Dio, di me!)

ALFREDO (*al Barone*)

Se continuar v'aggrada -

BARONE

Per ora nol possiamo:
più tardi la rivincita.

ALFREDO

Al giuoco che vorrete.

BARONE

Seguiam gli amici; poscia -

ALFREDO

Sarò qual bramerete - Andiam.

BARONE

Andiam.

FLORA

Let us go.

CHORUS (*moving towards the table*)

Let us go.

VIOLETTA

(What will happen? I shall die? Take pity,
dear God, take pity on me!)

ALFREDO (*aside, to the Baron*)

If you wish to continue -

BARON

We cannot, for the moment;
we'll play again, later.

ALFREDO

At any game you like.

BARON

Let us follow our friends; later -

ALFREDO

As you wish - let's go.

BARON

Let's go.

(*All go out through the centre door; for a moment the scene is deserted. Then Violetta returns, distressed.*)

Violetta and Alfredo confront one another over a taut musical accompaniment which reflects his insanely jealous bravado.

VIOLETTA

Invitato a qui seguirmi,
verrà desso? Vorrà udirmi?
Ei verrà, ché l'odio atroce
puote in lui più di mia voce.

ALFREDO

Mi chiamaste? Che bramate?

VIOLETTA

Questi luoghi abbandonate,
un periglio vi sovrasta -

ALFREDO

Ah, comprendo! Basta, basta.
E sì vile mi credete?

VIOLETTA

Ah no, no mai -

ALFREDO

Ma che temete?

VIOLETTA

Tremo sempre del barone.

ALFREDO

È fra noi mortal quistione -
s'ei cadrà per mano mia
un sol colpo vi torria
coll'amante il protettore.
V'atterrisce tal sciagura?

VIOLETTA

I invited him to follow me.
Will he come? Will he listen to me?
He will come, for his bitter hatred
will bring him, if not my voice.

ALFREDO

You called me? What do you want?

VIOLETTA

Please leave here at once.
You are in danger.

ALFREDO

Ah, I understand! Enough -
do you think I am such a coward?

VIOLETTA

Ah, no, no, never -

ALFREDO

What are you afraid of?

VIOLETTA

I am afraid of the Baron.

ALFREDO

There is bad blood between us -
if he falls into my hands,
a single blow will take away
your lover and your protector.
Would such a misfortune frighten you?

117

VIOLETTA

Ma s'ei fosse l'uccisore?
Ecco l'unica sventura -
ch'io pavento a me fatale!

ALFREDO

La mia morte! Che ven cale?

VIOLETTA

Deh, partite, e sull'istante.

ALFREDO

Partirò, ma giura innante
che dovunque seguirai
i passi miei.

VIOLETTA

Ah, no, giammai.

ALFREDO

No! giammai?

VIOLETTA

Va', sciagurato
scorda un nome ch'è infamato.
Va' - mi lascia sul momento -
di fuggirti un giuramento sacro io feci.

ALFREDO

A chi? dillo - chi potea?

VIOLETTA

A chi dritto pien n'avea.

VIOLETTA

But if he should kill you?
That is the only misfortune
which I fear - for it would kill me too!

ALFREDO

My death! What do you care?

VIOLETTA

Ah, leave, leave this minute!

ALFREDO

I shall leave, but first swear
that you will follow me
wherever I go.

VIOLETTA

Ah, no, never.

ALFREDO

No! Never?

VIOLETTA

Go wretched man!
Forget a name which is dishonoured.
Go - leave me this instant -
I took a sacred oath to leave you.

ALFREDO

But who - who could ask it of you?

VIOLETTA

Someone who had full right.

ALFREDO
Fu Douphol?

VIOLETTA
Sì.

ALFREDO
Dunque l'ami?

VIOLETTA
Ebben - l'amo -

ALFREDO

(In a blind fury he runs to the door and calls out.)

Or tutti a me.

(All the guests, bewildered, return to the salon.)

TUTTI
Ne appellaste? Che volete?

ALFREDO

(pointing to Violetta, who is leaning against the table in utter humiliation)

Questa donna conoscete?

TUTTI
Chi? Violetta?

ALFREDO
Che facesse non sapete?

ALFREDO
Was it Douphol?

VIOLETTA
Yes.

ALFREDO
You love him, then?

VIOLETTA
Well - I love him, yes.

ALFREDO

Everyone - come here!

ALL
You called us? What do you want?

ALFREDO

You know this woman?

ALL
Who? Violetta?

ALFREDO
You don't know what she has done?

VIOLETTA

Ah, taci.

VIOLETTA

Ah, be silent.

TUTTI

No.

ALL

No.

> **DISC NO. 2/TRACK 10**

Alfredo curses Violetta in a brief aria over a cabaletta-style figure in the orchestra. The guests respond wildly (00:58), their incredulity underlined by an unresolved closing chord.

ALFREDO

Ogni suo aver tal femmina
per amor mio sperdea.
Io cieco, vile, misero,
tutto accettar potea.
Ma è tempo ancora! Tergermi
da tanta macchia bramo.
Qui testimon vi chiamo
che qui pagato io l'ho.

ALFREDO

This woman was about to lose
all she owns for love of me;
while I, blinded, vile, wretched,
was capable of accepting everything.
But there is still time! I wish
to cleanse myself of such a stain.
I have called you here as witnesses
that I have paid her all I owe.

(With furious contempt, he throws a purse down at Violetta's feet. Violetta faints in the arms of Flora. As Alfredo is speaking the last few words, his father enters.)

TUTTI

Oh, infamia orribile tu commettesti!
Un cor sensibile così uccidesti!
Di donne ignobile insultatore,
di qui allontanati, ne desti orror!
Va', va', ne desti orror!
Di donne ignobile insultator, *ecc.*

ALL

Oh, what a terrible thing you have done!
You have killed a sensitive heart!
Ignoble man, to insult a woman so,
leave this house at once, you fill us with
horror! Go, go, you fill us with horror!
Ignoble man, to insult a woman, *etc.*

As with all of Germont's music, he responds here in expansive fatherly phrases. Alfredo, realizing what he has done, responds in halting phrases (00:50) as he tries to excuse his actions.

GERMONT

Di sprezzo degno sé stesso rende
chi pur nell'ira la donna offende.
Dov'è mio figlio? Più non lo vedo:
in te più Alfredo trovar non so.

ALFREDO

Ah, sì - che feci! Ne sento orrore.
Gelosa smania, deluso amore
mi strazian l'alma; più non ragiono.
Da lei perdono più non avrò.
Volea fuggirla - non ho potuto!
Dall'ira spinto son qui venuto!
Or che lo sdegno ho disfogato,
me sciagurato! rimorso n'ho.

TUTTI (a Violetta)

Oh, quanto peni! Ma pur fa cor.
Qui soffre ognuno del tuo dolor;
fra cari amici qui sei soltanto;
rasciuga il pianto che t'inondò.

GERMONT (da sé)

Io sol fra tanti so qual virtude
di quella misera il sen racchiude.
Io so che l'ama, che gli è fedele,
eppur crudele tacer dovrò!

GERMONT

Whoever, even in anger, offends a woman
exposes himself to the contempt of all.
Where is my son? I cannot find him,
for in you I no longer see Alfredo.

ALFREDO

Ah, yes - what have I done? I am horrified.
Maddening jealousy, disillusioned love
torture my heart - I have lost my reason.
She can never forgive me now,
I tried to flee from her - I couldn't!
I came here, spurred on by anger!
Now that I have vented my fury,
I am sick with remorse - oh, wretched man!

ALL (to Violetta)

Ah, how you suffer! But take heart,
here, each of us suffers for your sorrow;
you are here among dear friends;
dry the tears which bathe your face.

GERMONT (to himself)

I alone among these people know
what virtue there is in this poor woman's
heart. I know she loves him, is faithful to
him, and yet I must keep a pitiless silence!

BARONE *(piano, ad Alfredo)*
A questa donna l'atroce insulto
qui tutti offese, ma non inulto
fia tanto oltraggio - provar vi voglio
che il vostro orgoglio fiaccar saprò.

BARON *(in a low voice, to Alfredo)*
The atrocious insult to this woman
has shocked us all, but such an outrage
shall not go unavenged. I will show you
that I am well able to break your pride.

ALFREDO *(da sé)*
Ohimé, che feci! Ne sento orrore, *ecc.*
Da lei perdono più non avrò.

ALFREDO *(to himself)*
Alas, what have I done, *etc.*
I am horrified she can never forgive me now.

DISC NO. 2/TRACK 12

This large ensemble, in which everyone expresses their various thoughts at once, brings the act to a stunning conclusion. This convention of nineteenth-century opera does not advance the drama in real time, but allows us to dissect a climactic moment into its various components. Violetta begins in a distant voice, yet is always at the center of the vocal tableau, and builds to an emotional climax while audibly affecting those around her.

VIOLETTA *(riavendosi)*
Alfredo, Alfredo, di questo core
non puoi comprendere tutto l'amore;
tu non conosci che fino a prezzo
del tuo disprezzo provato io l'ho!

VIOLETTA *(regaining consciousness)*
Alfredo, Alfredo you cannot understand
fully the love I have in my heart;
you do not know that even at the risk
of your disdain I have put it to the test!

TUTTI *(a Violetta)*
Quanto peni! fa cor

ALL *(to Violetta)*
How you suffer! But take heart!

ALFREDO
Ohimè! che feci! Ne sento orror!

ALFREDO
Alas, what have I done? I am horrified!

VIOLETTA
Ma verrà tempo in che il saprai -
come t'amassi confesserai.
Dio dai rimorsi ti salvi allora, ah!
Io spenta ancora pur t'amerò.

VIOLETTA
But the day will come when you will know -
You will admit how much I loved you.
May God save you, then, from remorse,
I shall be dead, but I shall love you still.

ALFREDO

Ohimè! che feci! Ne sento orror!

BARONE

Provar vi voglio che tanto
orgoglio fiaccar saprò.

GERMONT

Io so che l'ama, che gli è fedele,
eppur crudele tacer dovrò!

TUTTI

Quanto peni! fa cor! *ecc.*

ALFREDO

Alas, what have I done? I am horrified!

BARON

I will show you that I am well able
to break your pride.

GERMONT

I know she loves him, is faithful to him,
and yet I must keep a pitiless silence!

ALL

How you suffer! Take heart! *etc.*

(Germont leads his son away with him; the Baron follows him. Flora and the Doctor accompany Violetta to her room. The others go out.)

Act 3

Violetta's bedroom. Upstage, a bed with half-drawn curtains; a window with inside shutters; next to the bed a low table with a water-bottle, a glass, various medicines. Downstage, a dressing-table; nearby a sofa; another table with a night-lamp; several chairs and other pieces. The door is to the left; opposite, a fireplace, with a low fire.

(Violetta is in bed, asleep. Annina, sitting in a chair near the fireplace, has dozed off.)

DISC NO. 2/TRACK 13

The Prelude begins with the same sorrowful music we heard in the Prelude to act I. This is followed by an extended lament which seems to express the alternating hope and despair of Violetta's situation.

DISC NO. 2/TRACK 14

The orchestra is muted and Violetta's lines are likewise quiet in this passage. She is barely alive.

VIOLETTA
Annina?

ANNINA
Comandate?

VIOLETTA
Dormivi, poveretta?

VIOLETTA
Annina?

ANNINA
Yes, madam?

VIOLETTA
Were you sleeping, poor child?

ANNINA	**ANNINA**
Sì, perdonate.	Yes. Forgive me.
VIOLETTA	**VIOLETTA**
Dammi d'acqua un sorso.	Give me a sip of water.
(Annina does so.)	
Osserva, è pieno il giorno?	Look outside and tell me - is it still day?
ANNINA	**ANNINA**
Son sett'ore.	It's seven o'clock.
VIOLETTA	**VIOLETTA**
Dà accesso a un po' di luce.	Open the blinds a little.
(Annina opens the blinds and looks out into the street.)	
ANNINA	**ANNINA**
Il signor di Grenvil!	Doctor Grenvil!
VIOLETTA	**VIOLETTA**
Oh, il vero amico!	Oh, he's a true friend!
Alzar mi vo' - m'aita.	I want to get up. Help me.

(She gets up then falls back on the bed. Finally, supported by Annina, she gets up and walks slowly to the sofa. The doctor enters in time to help her get comfortable. Annina brings cushions and puts them behind her.)

VIOLETTA	**VIOLETTA**
Quanta bontà!	How good you are!
pensaste a me per tempo!	you thought of me in time!
DOTTORE *(Le tocca il polso.)*	**DOCTOR** *(feeling her pulse)*
Sì, come vi sentite?	Yes. How do you feel?

VIOLETTA

Soffre il mio corpo.

Ma tranquilla ho l'alma.

Mi confortò ier sera un pio ministro.

Ah, religione è sollievo ai sofferenti.

DOTTORE

E questa notte?

VIOLETTA

Ebbi tranquillo il sonno.

DOTTORE

Coraggio adunque - la convalescenza
non è lontana.

VIOLETTA

Oh, la bugia pietosa
ai medici è concessa.

DOTTORE (*Le stringe la mano.*)
Addio - a più tardi.

VIOLETTA

Non mi scordate.

ANNINA

(*in a low voice, as she shows the doctor out*)

Come va, signore?

DOTTORE

La tisi non le accorda che poche ore.

VIOLETTA

My body suffers, but my soul is in peace.
Last evening a priest came to comfort me.
Religion is a great consolation to the
suffering.

DOCTOR

And during the night?

VIOLETTA

I slept quite peacefully.

DOCTOR

Courage, then. Your convalescence is not
far off.

VIOLETTA

Oh, the little white lie
is permissible in a doctor.

DOCTOR (*pressing her hand*)
Goodbye - I'll come back later.

VIOLETTA

Don't forget me.

ANNINA

How is she, sir?

DOCTOR

She has only a few hours to live.

ANNINA

Or fate cor.

VIOLETTA

Giorno di festa è questo?

ANNINA

Tutta Parigi impazza - è carnevale!

VIOLETTA

Ah, nel comun tripudio, sallo Iddio
quanti infelici soffron! Quale somma
v'ha in quello stipo?

(pointing)

ANNINA

(opening the drawer and counting the money)

Venti luigi.

VIOLETTA

Dieci ne reca a' poveri tu stessa.

ANNINA

Poco rimanvi allora -

VIOLETTA

Oh, mi saran bastanti.
Cerca poscia mie lettere.

ANNINA

Ma voi?

ANNINA

Take heart, now.

VIOLETTA

Today is a holiday?

ANNINA

Paris is going mad - it's carnival.

VIOLETTA

Oh, in all this merrymaking, heaven knows
how many poor ones are suffering! How much
is there in that drawer?

ANNINA

Twenty louis.

VIOLETTA

Take ten and give them to the poor.

ANNINA

There won't be much left -

VIOLETTA

Oh, for me it will be enough.
Then bring in my letters.

ANNINA

But you, madam?

VIOLETTA

Nulla occorrà - sollecita, se puoi.

VIOLETTA

Nothing will happen - go quickly, please.

(Annina goes out.)

VIOLETTA

VIOLETTA

(She takes a letter from her bosom and reads:)

DISC NO. 2/TRACK 15

Violetta speaks the words of the letter over a solo violin echoing the love theme from act 1. This technique has since been abused by many movies, but remains striking in this context.

"Teneste la promessa - la disfida ebbe luogo! Il Barone fu ferito però migliora. Alfredo è in stranio suolo; il vostro sacrifizio io stesso gli ho svelato; egli a voi tornerà pel suo perdono; io pur verrò. Curatevi - mertate un avvenir migliore. Giorgio Germont."
È tardi!
Attendo, attendo - né a me giungon mai!

"You kept your promise. The duel has taken place! The Baron was wounded, but is recovering. Alfredo has gone abroad; I myself revealed your sacrifice to him; he will return to ask your pardon; I too shall come. Take care of yourself. You deserve a happier future. Giorgio Germont."
It is late!
I wait, I wait - they never come to me!

(She looks at herself in the mirror.)

DISC NO. 2/TRACK 16

Addio del passato. This famous aria is a masterpiece of construction. Introduced by a melancholy solo oboe, Violetta's farewells are accompanied by halting figures in the orchestra that call to mind her shortness of breath. As she recalls Alfredo's love (00:58) her lines begin to soar, and as she prays for redemption the orchestra presses forward in an ascending harmonic progression (02:05) Having expended all her energies, her line descends, punctuated by isolated chords in the strings, and she ends on an unaccompanied high A (03:26).

Oh, come son mutata!
Ma il dottore a sperar pure m'esorta!
Ah, con tal morbo ogni speranza è morta.
Addio, del passato bei sogni ridenti,
le rose del volto già sono pallenti;
l'amore d'Alfredo perfino mi manca,
conforto, sostegno dell'anima stanca -
conforto, sostegno -
Ah, della traviata sorridi al desio;
a lei, deh, perdona; tu accoglila, o Dio!
Ah! - Tutto,
tutto finì, or tutto, tutto finì.

Ah, how I have changed!
But the doctor still gives me hope!
Ah, with this disease every hope is dead.
Adieu, sweet, happy dreams of the past,
the roses of my cheeks are already fading.
I miss so much Alfredo's love,
which once solaced my weary soul -
Solaced and comforted -
Ah, smile upon the woman who has
strayed; forgive her, oh God, grant she may
come to thee!
Now all is finished, all is over.

DISC NO. 2/TRACK 17
The revelers outside underline the marked contrast between Violetta's former life and the darkened room in which she now awaits her death.

CORO DI MASCHERE
(dall'esterno)
Largo al quadrupede sir della festa,
di fiori e pampini
cinta la testa.
Largo al piu dociled'ogni cornuto,
di corni e pifferi abbia il saluto.
Parigini, date passo, al trionfo del Bue grasso. L'Asia né l'Africa
vide il più bello, vanto ed orgoglio d'ogni
macello. Allegre maschere, pazzi garzoni,
tutti plauditelo con canti e suoni!
Parigini, date passo,
al trionfo del Bue grasso.
Largo al quadrupede sir della festa,
di fiori e pampini
cinta la testa.

CHORUS OF MASQUERADERS
(from the street)
Make way for the quadruped King of the
festival, Wearing his crown of flowers
and vine leaves. Make way for the tamest of
all who wear horns, greet him with music
of horn and flute. People of Paris,
open the path to the triumphant Fattened
Ox. Neither Asia nor Africa
has ever seen better, this pride and joy of
the butcher's trade. Light-hearted maidens,
and frolicking lads, pay him due honour
of music and song! People of Paris, open
the path to the triumphant Fattened Ox.
Make way for the quadruped King of the
festival wearing his crown of flowers
and vine leaves.

(Annina returns, hastily.)

The excitement moves inside as Annina enters. The harmonies remain unstable—their direction uncertain—until we hear the news of Alfredo's imminent return, and all resolves in an optimistic major key.

ANNINA *(esitando)*
Signora!

ANNINA *(hesitating)*
Madam!

VIOLETTA
Che t'accadde?

VIOLETTA
What has happened?

ANNINA
Quest'oggi, è vero, vi sentite meglio?

ANNINA
Today you feel better, don't you?

VIOLETTA
Sì, perché?

VIOLETTA
Yes. Why?

ANNINA
D'esser calma promettete?

ANNINA
Do you promise not to get excited?

VIOLETTA
Sì, che vuoi dirmi?

VIOLETTA
Yes. What do you want to tell me?

ANNINA
Prevenir vi volli -
un gioia improvvisa!

ANNINA
I wanted to prepare you -
A happy surprise!

VIOLETTA
Una gioia! Dicesti?

VIOLETTA
Did you say - a surprise?

ANNINA
Sì, o signora -

ANNINA
Oh yes, madam -

VIOLETTA
Alfredo! Ah, tu il vedesti?
Ei vien! T'affretta.

VIOLETTA
Alfredo! Ah, you saw him?
He is coming! Oh, quickly!

(Annina nods her head, then goes to open the door.)

Alfredo!   Alfredo!

(Alfredo enters, pale with emotion. They are in each other's arms as they exclaim:)

Amato Alfredo! Oh gioia!   Beloved Alfredo! Oh joy!

ALFREDO   **ALFREDO**
Oh mia Violetta. Oh gioia!   My Violetta! Oh, joy!
Colpevol sono - so tutto,   The fault is mine - I know everything now,
o cara.   dear.

VIOLETTA   **VIOLETTA**
Io so che alfine reso mi sei!   I know only that you have come back!

ALFREDO   **ALFREDO**
Da questo palpito s'io t'ami impara,   Let my emotion teach you how I love you.
senza te esistere più non potrei.   I cannot live without you.

VIOLETTA   **VIOLETTA**
Ah, s'anco in vita m'hai ritrovata,   Ah, if you have found me still alive,
credi che uccidere non può il dolor.   it means grief has not the power to kill.

ALFREDO   **ALFREDO**
Scorda l'affanno, donna adorata,   Forget your sorrow, my adored one,
a me perdona e al genitor.   and forgive my father and me.

VIOLETTA   **VIOLETTA**
Ch'io ti perdoni? La rea son io;   What is there to forgive? The guilty one is
ma solo amor tal mi rendé.   me; but it was love alone which made me so.

ALFREDO, VIOLETTA   **ALFREDO, VIOLETTA**
Null'uomo o demon, angel mio,   Now neither man nor demon, my angel,
mai più dividermi potrà da te.   will ever be able to take you away.

Parigi, o cara. **This famous duet, in which the lovers describe an idyllic future together, is often performed in concert. The music is perfectly symmetrical and marvelously intertwined between the two lovers. They are finally together in every sense, but it is too late for them.**

ALFREDO

Parigi, o cara, noi lasceremo,
la vita uniti trascorreremo;
de' corsi affanni compenso avrai,
la tua salute rifiorirà.
Sospiro e luce tu mi sarai,
tutto il futuro ne arriderà.

VIOLETTA

(echoing him as in a dream)

Parigi, o caro, noi lasceremo,
la vita uniti trascorreremo:

ALFREDO

Sì.
De' corsi affanni compenso avrai.
La tua salute rifiorirà.
Sospiro e luce tu mi sarai, *ecc.*

ALFREDO

From Paris dear, we shall go away,
to live our lives together.
We shall make up for all our heartache,
your health will come back again.
You will be the light of my life,
the future will smile upon us.

VIOLETTA

From Paris dear, we shall go away,
to live our loves together…

ALFREDO

Yes.
We shall make up for all our heartache.
Your health will come back again.
You will be the light of my life, *etc.*

We hear Violetta's heart beat faster as she tries to take up her life again, but the low strings repeatedly interject short descending phrases which punctuate her failures.

VIOLETTA

Ah, non più, a un tempio -
Alfredo, andiamo,
del tuo ritorno grazie rendiamo.

VIOLETTA

No more now, Alfredo let us go to church
to offer thanks
for your return.

(She sways, as if to fall.)

ALFREDO
Tu impallidisci -

ALFREDO
You are pale -

VIOLETTA
È nulla, sai!
Gioia improvvisa non entra mai,
senza turbarlo, in mesto core.

VIOLETTA
It is nothing!
Such sudden joy cannot come
to a sorrowing heart without disturbing it.

(She throws herself down, upon a chair; her head falls back.)

ALFREDO *(spaventato, sorreggendola)*
Gran Dio! Violetta!

ALFREDO *(holding her up, terrified)*
Great God! Violetta!

VIOLETTA *(sforzandosi)*
È il mio malore -
fu debolezza! Ora son forte.
Vedi? Sorrido.

VIOLETTA *(with great effort)*
It's my illness -
A moment of weakness! Now I am strong.
See? I am smiling.

ALFREDO
Ahi, cruda sorte!

ALFREDO
Ah, cruel destiny!

VIOLETTA
Fu nulla. Annina, dammi a vestire.

VIOLETTA
It was nothing. Annina, bring me my dress.

ALFREDO
Adesso? Attendi.

ALFREDO
Now? Wait.

VIOLETTA
No - voglio uscire.

VIOLETTA
No. I want to go out.

(Annina gives her a dress which she tries to put on. Too weak to succeed, she exclaims:)

Gran Dio! Non posso!

Dear God! I cannot!

ALFREDO

(Cielo! Che vedo!)

(to Annina)

Va' pel dottore.

VIOLETTA

Ah! Digli che Alfredo
è ritornato all'amor mio -
Digli che vivere ancor vogl'io.

(Annina goes out. Then, to Alfredo:)

ALFREDO

(Heaven! What is this!)

Go to call the doctor.

VIOLETTA

Tell him that Alfredo
has come back to his love.
Tell him I want to live again.

DISC 2/TRACKS 21 & 22

Violetta realizes the seriousness of her condition, and her music takes on a martial tone, as if she is rebelling aginst fate. Germont's return cheers her slightly but only briefly.

Ma se tornando non m'hai salvato,
a niuno in terra salvarmi è dato.
Ah! gran Dio! Morir sì giovine,
io che penato ho tanto!
Morir sì presso a tergere
il mio sì lungo pianto!
Ah, dunque fu delirio
la credula speranza;
invano di costanza
armato avrò il mio cor!

If in returning you have not saved my life,
then nothing on earth can save me.
Ah! Dear God! To die so young.
when I have sorrowed so long!
To die, when now, at last,
I might have ceased my weeping!
Ah, it was but a dream,
my credulous hope;
to sheathe my heart in constancy
was all in vain.

ALFREDO

Oh mio sospiro e palpito,
diletto del cor mio!
Le mie colle tue lagrime
confondere degg'io -

ALFREDO

My very breath of life, sweet
pulse of my heart!
My tears must flow
together with yours.

Ma più che mai, deh credilo,
m'è d'uopo di costanza.
Ah, tutto alla speranza
non chiudere il tuo cor.
Ah! Violetta mia, deh calmati,
m'uccide il tuo dolor deh, calmati!

But more than ever, ah, believe me,
we have need of constancy.
Ah! Do not close
your heart to hope.
Ah, my Violetta, be calm,
you grief is killing me, be calm!

VIOLETTA
Oh Alfredo! il crudo termine
serbato al nostro amor!

VIOLETTA
Oh, Alfredo, what a cruel end
for our love!

(Violetta sinks down upon the sofa. Germont enters, followed after a moment by Dr. Grenvil.)

GERMONT
Ah, Violetta!

GERMONT
Ah, Violetta!

VIOLETTA
Voi, signor!

VIOLETTA
You, sir!

ALFREDO
Mio padre!

ALFREDO
Father!

VIOLETTA
Non mi scordaste?

VIOLETTA
You had not forgotten me?

GERMONT
La promessa adempio.
A stringervi qual figlia vengo al seno,
o generosa!

GERMONT
I am fulfilling my promise.
I have come to embrace you as a daughter.
O generous woman!

VIOLETTA
Ahimè, tardi giungeste!

VIOLETTA
Alas, you have come too late!

(She embraces him.)

Pure, grate ven sono.
Grenvil, vedete? Fra le braccia io spiro
di quanti cari ho al mondo.

But I am grateful to you.
Grenvil, see? I am dying in the arms
of the only dear ones I have.

GERMONT

Che mai dite!
(Oh cielo - è ver!)

GERMONT

What are you saying!
(Oh, heaven, it is true!)

ALFREDO

La vedi, padre mio?

ALFREDO

Do you see her, father?

GERMONT

Di più non lacerarmi.
Troppo rimorso l'alma mi divora.
Quasi fulmin m'atterra ogni suo detto.
Oh, malcauto vegliardo!
Il mal ch'io feci ora sol vedo!

GERMONT

Don't torture me any longer.
My soul is already devoured by remorse.
Every word she speaks is a thunderbolt.
Oh, rash old man!
Only now do I see the harm I have done.

VIOLETTA

VIOLETTA

(Meanwhile, with great difficulty, she has opened a secret drawer of her dressing table. She takes from it a medallion and gives it to Alfredo.)

DISC NO. 2/TRACK 23

Finally resigned to her fate, Violetta gives her medallion to Alfredo over a funeral march motive in the orchestra which becomes more insistent as Alfredo and his father pour out their despair. As Violetta slips away, the key becomes major (01:07), but it is still punctuated by the funereal figure—we hear both heaven and earth. Over shimmering strings, a solo violin once again announces the love theme (03:22). It grows in intensity as she rallies one last time, and at the peak of her ecstasy, she falls dead and the orchestra hurdles toward its final tragic D-flat minor chord.

Più a me t'appressa -
Ascolta, amato Alfredo.

Come nearer to me -
Listen, beloved Alfredo.

Prendi, quest'è l'immagine de' miei passati
giorni; a rammentarti torni
colei che sì t'amò.

ALFREDO
No, non morrai, non dirmelo -
Dei viver, amor mio.
A strazio sì terribil
qui non mi trasse Iddio.

GERMONT
Cara, sublime, sublime vittima
d'un disperato amore,
perdonami lo strazio recato al tuo bel cor.

VIOLETTA
Se una pudica vergine degli anni suoi sul
fiore, a te donasse il core -
sposa ti sia - lo vo'.
Le porgi quest'effigie;
dille che dono ell'è di chi nel ciel tra gli
angeli prega per lei, per te.

GERMONT
Finché avrà il ciglio lagrime
io piangerò per te.
Vola a' beati spiriti,
Iddio ti chiama a sé.

ALFREDO
Sì presto, ah no, dividerti
morte non può da me.
Ah, vivi, o solo un feretro
m'accoglierà con te.

Take this, it is a portrait painted some years
ago. It will help you to remember
the one who loved you so.

ALFREDO
Ah, you will not die, don't tell me so -
You must live, my darling.
God did not bring me back to you
to face such a tragedy.

GERMONT
Dear noble victim of a hopeless love,
forgive me for having made your heart
suffer.

VIOLETTA
If some young girl in the flower of life
should give her heart to you - marry her -
wish it. Then give her this portrait:
Tell her it is the gift of one who, in heaven
among the angels, prays for her and for you.

GERMONT
As long as my eyes have tears,
so long shall I weep for you.
Fly to the realm of the blessed,
God calls you unto him.

ALFREDO
So soon, oh no, death
cannot take you from me.
Ah, live, or a single coffin
will receive me as well as you.

VIOLETTA *(rianimata)*
È strano!
Cessarono gli spasimi del dolore.
In me rinasce - m'agita insolito vigor!
Ah! ma io ritorno a viver!
Oh gioia!

(She falls down, senseless, upon the sofa.)

FINE

VIOLETTA *(getting up, as if reinvigorated)*
How strange!
The spasms of pain have ceased:
A strange vigour has brought me to life!
Ah! I shall live -
Oh, joy!

END

LA TRAVIATA

Giuseppe Verdi

COMPACT DISC ONE   67:32:00

1	Prelude	4:31

ATTO PRIMO/ACT ONE

2	Dell'invito tracorsa è gia l'ora	5:02
3	Libiamo ne'lieti calici	3:02
	Alfredo/Violetta	
4	Che è ciò?	2:24
5	Un dì, felice eterea	3:33
	Alfredo/Violetta	
6	Ebben? Che diavol fate?	1:27
7	Si ridesta in ciel l'aurora	1:53
	tutti	
8	È strano	1:28
	Violetta	
9	Ah, fors'è lui	5:59
	Violetta	
10	Follie! Follie!	1:15
	Violetta	
11	Sempre libera	3:49
	Violetta	

ATTO SECONDO/ACT TWO

COMPACT DISC TWO 70:26:00

ATTO TERZO/ACT THREE